UNITED METHODIST DOCTRINE

Thomas F. Chilcote

DISCIPLESHIP RESOURCES
MATERIALS FOR GROWTH IN CHRISTIAN FAITH AND LIFE

P.O. Box 189 • Nashville, TN 37202 • Phone (615) 340-7285

Library of Congress Catalog Card No. 89-51191

ISBN 0-88177-080-9

All scripture quotations are taken from the Revised Standard Version of the Holy Bible.

DR080B

CONTENTS

INTRODUCTION

Those of us who live in the United States are sometimes chided by our friends in other parts of the world for being activists who do not have any particular interest in doctrinal matters. The locale in which we live and work always affects our thinking and conduct, but we cannot forget that we also live in the mainstream of Wesleyan doctrinal tradition. Wesley, too, was an activist! Robert Browning's familiar lines written in 1841 strike us as being romantic rather than realistic. In his poem, "Pippa Passes," he wrote:

> God's in his heaven;
> All's right with the world.

How could Browning have insulated himself from the tragic events of his time? Many of them involved his own country, England: the Opium War in China, the forceful putting down of the Afghan revolt against British rule, the war between China and Britain, the Irish revolt against England, the war between India and England. And elsewhere: the French conquests of Algiers and Morocco, the United States-Mexican War, and the great Irish Famine—all of these events were crowded into the span of six years, 1840-1846.

Nor could anyone in that day who was attuned to the times have missed John Stuart Mill's assessment of the immense social harm that accompanied the Industrial Revolution—men and women, even children, working long hours in unsanitary, ill-ventilated factories, living in crowded slums, with unregulated industry completely unconcerned about the most basic human rights.

WESLEY'S ENGLAND

A century earlier England could not take pride in conditions the political power structure allowed to prevail. John Wesley called on

English men and women to open their eyes. He knew that if they looked around they would see darkness thick enough to be felt. They would see ignorance and error. Vice, along with consciousness of guilt, fear, sorrow, shame, and remorse, was epidemic. Misery, sickness, and pain haunted the whole world. The poor and the helpless faced desperation every day.

We cannot imagine one of the pastimes of that period. It consisted of visitors standing outside the windows of asylums where the spectators could watch the pathetic antics of the insane. This amusement became so popular that many thousands indulged in it, and the fee they paid became an important source of institutional revenue!

Even education had fallen on hard times. Students at Oxford University, according to Adam Smith (a contemporary of the Wesleys), were lazy and shiftless. The professors scoffed at teaching. Discipline was lax to make it easy on those who were "in charge." People freely indulged in drinking and gambling. One Oxford tutor was remembered by one of his students as a man who received a salary but performed no duties. That student looked back on the years he spent there as the most idle and unprofitable period of his life. Those who heard Wesley preach at the university were annoyed and embarrassed, and blushed to think that so able a Fellow should exhibit such bad taste as to take God so seriously and publicly before an enlightened audience.

As for the established church, Wesley believed that its leaders were "rethinking Christianity downward," leaving the chief doctrines of Christian perfection and the gospel of saving faith in shreds and patches. Instead, they proclaimed an easy ascent of human thought and conduct from humanity to God. A staunch Anglican bishop regretfully acknowledged that the decay of religion was widespread and everyone could see it.

COMPLEXITIES IN AMERICAN CULTURE

What about American society in our time? Are we able to address our culture in any persuasive way with regard to Christian ideals and expectations? We all know the scene quite well: the nuclear arms threat; explosions in communications, technology, population, hunger, and knowledge; the saturation of everyday life with entertainment, sports, recreation; unimaginable affluence; the precariousness of family life, immorality, compromised ethics in politics and business; and the pervasiveness of secularism. Focusing on a few illustrations will sharpen the picture.

Violence among families has reached horrifying proportions. The 456,000 annually reported cases of disorder do not include thousands of other acts of violence that are unreported because the victims are either embarrassed or feel hopeless about the possibility of stopping the abuse.

Consider the increasing number of suicides in American society. Suicides now exceed homicides. Approximately 30,000 persons commit suicide each year in the United States—5,000 of them adolescents—with 250,000 attempts. Reasons given for this high and increasing incidence of suicide among teenagers are many: a saturation of the job market, families in fragmented disarray, both parents working, a sense of hopelessness, role models reflecting personal desperation, increased incidence of drug and alcohol abuse, promiscuity that damages self-esteem, a decline in religious values with increasing difficulty in being a religious person. Among older persons, reasons include the feeling that "life is over for me," chronic sickness and pain, loneliness and abandonment by families, and dwindling financial resources. This overview of life is not a bright picture at all.

Individuals, even those who are in our churches, are finding it difficult to get a satisfying direction for a meaningful life. The church, not of its own choosing, must engage in a running battle against an array of self-help movements, some of them in religious disguise. These movements, even after they have run their course, leave their "disciples" disillusioned, disenchanted, and, to use Albert Outler's words, "sadly vulnerable to secular tyranny."

THE CHURCH VERSUS THE CULTURE

Pastors and church members are understandably obligated to maintain internal tranquility and multiple ministries to serve their congregations. However, these heavy demands allow little time or energy to reach out to that increasingly large segment of the community beyond the established fellowship. The unreached in our immediate communities comprise the church's home mission field.

We realistically build sanctuaries to accommodate no more than one-third of our anticipated membership, and even at that, pews remain empty. We feel obligated to correct membership rosters periodically, but worry about taking such losses. When I served as a district superintendent, I asked the churches not to purge their rolls, but to give me a name for every number. I even provided forms for making the lists. In one relatively small congregation a woman who served on the committee to develop an accurate listing discovered that her name appeared five times!

Wesley was troubled about the spiritual bankruptcy of the Christianity of his age. He looked upon Anglicanism as the church of missed opportunities. Little is gained by speaking negatively about United Methodism in America today. Many are anxious about the state of the church.

Perhaps a service our bewildered and distraught age really wants us to provide is a simplification of what is most important—to give joy and meaning back to life. The once reliable traditions that gave society its spine and continuity have been crumbling. In fact, not long ago a book came off the press with the title, *The Age of Discontinuity*. We hear plenty about human self-sufficiency. God's overarching stake in our lives and culture is largely ignored. The time is now for the church to proclaim a God-centered message rather than a merely human-based message about life.

WESLEY'S "FOUR PILLARS"

To open up this issue, we might recover Wesley's four grand pillars on which he believed Christianity was built: the power, understanding, goodness, and holiness of God. On the other hand, we find three doctrines that bear directly upon our lives: original sin, justification by faith alone, and holiness of heart and life.

As we begin to interpret such straightforward doctrine as the key to life in its fullness, we may happily witness a restoration of spiritual joy and peace to drab and troubled hearts. We must encourage each person to believe only what he or she clearly understands, not pressing anyone to accept what he or she cannot comprehend.

CHRIST'S CENTRALITY AND ADEQUACY

As a final introductory issue, the centrality and adequacy of Jesus Christ needs to be highlighted. When I was under non-pastoral appointment for more than eleven years as a college president, I was cast more in the role of a layperson than of a pastor. I became a worshiper in the congregation rather than a proclaimer in the pulpit. I have listened to good men and women who, carefully and in good faith, explained biblical passages and interpreted events of our time in light of New Testament principles. I am sure that Christ was at the center of their conscientious preparation and delivery, but the exhilaration of Christ's lordship over their hearts seemed too often to be lacking. I do not say this as one who stands in harsh judgment over others. I cannot help but feel, however, that the pulpit so often fears fire or frost in religion—more probably afraid of fire than frost!

An Oxford (England) student took it upon himself in the early 1760s to examine the preaching in all the leading London pulpits. After doing so, he reported that he could not find in any one of the sermons any more of Christianity than could be found in the writings of Cicero; nor could he make out from the content of the preaching whether the preacher was a disciple of Confucius, Mohammed, or Christ.

We are engaged as individual believers and as the church in the unfinished work of Christ. Two descriptions of Christ's character and work gave Wesley an awareness of the urgency of giving him centrality in life. These two descriptions help us feel certainty as we present Christ in his beauty and splendor, believing he can and will draw persons to himself. John Wesley was distressed that so-called persons of quality were saying they could not see much need for Jesus Christ.

1. Wesley argued that Christ did nothing amiss. He was not guilty of any outward sin. He was pure in speech, never uttering an improper word. He indulged in no improper action. He expressed righteousness by doing all things well in obedience to the will of the Father who sent him. In fulfilling all righteousness he was compelled to endure suffering in order to keep his integrity.

2. Wesley recognized what might be called Christ's internal righteousness, the image of God stamped on Jesus' total character and

being. Divine righteousness was supremely imparted to his humanity. In him the divine purity, the divine justice, mercy, and truth, were joined. He demonstrated love, reverence, resignation to God, humility, meekness, gentleness, and compassion for lost humanity. All of this "righteousness" he reflected in the highest degree, without any defect.

This introduction points once more to the diversity and needs of our society. Secularism and materialism gravely threaten spiritual sensitivity and Christian nurture. The society we live in, the plight of the persons being addressed by the gospel, the anxieties and difficulties of the church as it tries to bring the good news to bear upon life, the clear message of the Christian faith, and the centrality and adequacy of Christ reaffirm deeply rooted beliefs, making them useful and perhaps urgent.

We turn now to consideration of the need for human redemption and how it can be gained—a cardinal doctrine of United Methodism.

CHAPTER ONE

THE PRECIOUSNESS OF LIFE

he judgment many of us put on our lives is, for the most part, unreliable. Our inclination is to think of ourselves more favorably than we ought to think (Romans 12:3). Realism begins to affect our judgment when we raise questions such as: What or who is God? Why *does* God or *should* God care about me? What has God done for me? Who am I?

Consider the marvel of the continuity of human life. How delicate it is! Even though each person's earthly existence is brief, divine providence provides renewable cells and such precious gifts as the ability to walk, speak, eat, and think.

HUMANITY AT THE APEX OF CREATION

In addition to such obvious physical benefits, human beings, unlike any other creatures, bear a unique likeness to the God who created us. The ancient Genesis hymns of creation rejoice in our being made unlike any other being. John Wesley talked about the original godlikeness of humanity, who did not know evil in any kind or degree. Like God, the first human being was inwardly and outwardly sinless and undefiled. A good God could not have created a being of less magnificence at the apex of creation.

Wesley also observed that humankind, in the beginning, was inclined only to good words and work and was capable of full and perfect

1

obedience to God's perfect law. Unlike other creatures, human beings are capable of knowing, loving, and obeying God. Like the Creator, we are furnished with understanding, will, and freedom to make choices.

God showed his desires for us by planting pure love in the human heart and clothing humankind with sinlessness, righteousness, and holiness. Such a creation was capable of entering into full fellowship with the divine. Little wonder that God, as the scriptures affirm, looked upon all creation, humankind included, and called it "very good."

HUMANITY'S CONTRARY NATURE

Sadly, this idyllic relationship took a tragic turn. Our first parents, as we regard the father (Adam) and mother (Eve) of all the human family, are represented in the Genesis story as wanting more than God gave them. They wanted to be not merely God-like but equal to God. They wanted to exercise all the power and comprehend all knowledge that, in this moral universe, had been reserved for the Creator alone.

So Eve flexed her self-will, disobeyed the divine expectation, and became aware of not only good, but evil. Nor was Adam more faithful to his Maker. He, too, chose to do his own will, rather than the will of the Creator. He knowingly and deliberately rebelled against God. In that moment he lost the divine moral image. So it came to pass that the children of God became spiritually bankrupt, separated and alienated from God. What has happened has been on humanity's initiative. God never desired or designed it.

For countless generations we have been wrestling with the tormenting problem of evil, which the late E. Stanley Jones pointed out is nothing less than "live" spelled backwards.

Methodism, from its Wesleyan beginnings, has acknowledged and accepted the scriptural interpretations and explanations of sin. Three important considerations are: (1) original sin, (2) persistent sin, and (3) universal sin.

Original sin

First, we consider *original sin*. Persons of ethical sensitivity have long perceived that infinite distance exists between the perfect holiness of God and the stricken state of humankind. They have also sensed that the alienation between God and humankind was not God's doing, but resulted from human arrogance and willful choice.

Wesley, reflecting on this early and tragic separation, believed that when Adam disobeyed God he was condemned by the righteous judgment of God. Immediately the sentence, of which he had been warned, began. Once he had eaten of the forbidden fruit, he began to die. His soul became separated from God and his body became corruptible and mortal.

This loss of divine character became human nature, affecting human reason as well as human will. No part of human nature was uninfected, and thereafter all persons born into the human family were mortal, disunited from God, inheritors of a sinful nature, and liable to death eternal (Romans 5:18; Ephesians 2:3). In these ways the sin of Adam and Eve became the sin of all humankind. Spiritual as well as temporal sorrow, pain, and death reversed the human condition from its likeness to God and the privileges of that exalted relationship.

"Original" sin is not an abstract speculation. It plagues us as agonizingly as it did Wesley. Something has gone terribly wrong. The signs of deep discrepancy between what human existence ought to be and what it actually is are everywhere and always visible.

Religious sentiment in the United States (and perhaps elsewhere) has for a long time raised doubts about the reality of sin, any kind of sin. We are more comfortable and feel less guilty when we talk about making mistakes or committing errors. The time has come to state clearly that the prayers of confession in services of public worship either address a real issue, or they are empty and meaningless ritual.

Persistent sin

Now consider *persistent sin*. We have no difficulty observing that even children of devout parents who earnestly do their best to help them live good and virtuous lives have a natural attraction to evil. A home that reflects a loving and moral environment cannot cancel out or ward off subtle and deep-seated rebelliousness in the children. We find it difficult not to believe that original sin is persistent and that it corrupts life from one generation to the next.

The seeds of sin take quick rootage. The branches spread rapidly and the fruits appear almost overnight. What branches grow from such an evil root? Among them we find first unbelief and then independence from God. These results are followed by pride, which foolishly insists on a need for nothing. The fruits growing on such branches are contention, vain boasting, and seeking and receiving praise, and have the effect of robbing God of the divine glory. Another fruit is the lust of the flesh that in various and many ways defiles the body designed to be God's temple. We also see the fruit of unbelief in evil and idle words and unholy deeds.

No matter how sincerely we may feel "heartily sorry" for having lost many a blessing, or how earnestly we may desire to break away from sin and even strive with all our might to regain our lost God-likeness, we are forced to conclude that we cannot win those victories by our own determination.

Sin is mightier than all our best intentions to free ourselves. We can resolve not to sin, yet we continue to sin. The more we wish, strive, and labor to be free of transgression, the more futile does the effort become. Desperation stalks our days. We toil tirelessly and endlessly, we repent and go on sinning; we pray and get no relief. Finally, as poor and sinful and helpless creatures, we reach our wits' end.

When we realize that we are hopelessly trapped in the web of persistent sin, we can no longer sing joyous redemption songs with any fervor. Our sin so haunts us that sermons or hymns that ought to lift our hearts no longer bless or inspire us.

Universal sin

Third, consider the *universality of sin*. This doctrine seems to be more offensive than either original or persistent sin. Many persons want to believe they are exempted from sin and its consequences. In Wesley's England, the Duchess of Buckingham, like many others, held herself in high personal esteem. She was accorded considerable public recognition because of her position in society and her respectable heredity. In a letter to the Countess of Huntingdon, a friend of John Wesley, she wrote that the Methodist doctrines were most repulsive and strongly tinctured with impertinence toward their superiors because they perpetually endeavored to level all ranks and do away with all distinctions. She said it was monstrous to be told that you have a heart as sinful as common wretches. She thought such notions were highly offensive and insulting, and could not understand why the Countess should entertain sentiments at such variance with her high rank and good breeding.

Every human being is equally precious in God's sight. Through pride, we set up idols in our hearts. We worship ourselves, our possessions, or even our God-given talents.

George Croft Cell, a Wesleyan scholar of a generation ago, pointed out that Wesley did not change his message whether he addressed sophisticated Oxford audiences or the working people of Cornwall, the miners at Kingswood, the shipbuilders at Newcastle, the drunkards of Moorefields, or the harlots of Drury Lane. He saw all of them as sinners in need of a savior, without any merit of their own, and with no resource but the grace of God. That was, to say the least, a humbling if not insulting doctrine.

UNIVERSAL DESTITUTION

So spiritual destitution is not merely to be found here and there. It is universal. In our alienation from God we are bound together in a democracy of disobedience. The scriptural revelation cannot be ignored. Sin is pervasive—always and everywhere present. All persons, high and low, the wealthy and the poor, the sophisticated and the crude, need to be delivered from the corruption and bondage that infect everyone.

Saint Paul, mindful of struggles of the spirit that he had to battle throughout his lifetime, always included himself among the sinful. His words sound like our own testimony:

I do not understand my own actions. For I do not do what I want, but I do the very thing I hate. Now if I do what I do not want, I agree that the law is good. So then it is no longer I that do it, but sin which dwells within me. For I know that nothing good dwells within me, that is, in my flesh. I can will what is right, but I cannot do it. For I do not do the good I want, but the evil I do not want is what I do. Now if I do what I do not want, it is no longer I that do it, but sin which dwells with me (Romans 7:15-20, RSV).

We resort to many justifications to reinforce our reluctance to get involved in a divine encounter that would, in fact, deliver us from spiritual slavery and restore us to our Father's affection. We can be encouraged by remembering Jesus' parable of the prodigal son (Luke 15:11-32). Consider the difficulty that runaway boy had in deciding to return to his father's house. Some excuses we conjure up to avoid returning to God are listed below:

Reconciliation will fail

We resist because we think a reconciliation would be too difficult and thus doomed to failure. It would expect too much, not only from us, but from God.

The late Bishop Gerald Kennedy sensed this. He understood that no real Christian ever talks about forgiveness as if it were something cheap and easy. He pointed out that the kind of person who says that it is God's business to forgive us and that we should take it without much ado is the kind of person who never experienced it. He made the crucial discovery that it is a terrible thing to be forgiven. He recognized that the defenses are all down and the soul stands stripped of its pride. So he concluded that the only possible comfort in the forgiveness of God is to surrender completely to God's will, which more times than not will insist on our taking up the cross.

The call is no longer compelling

Another hindrance is the notion that God's call through Christ came into the world so long ago and far away that it is no longer compelling and binding. Many persons who hear the gospel find it difficult to believe it and to apply it after two thousand years. We also find it difficult to believe that Jesus Christ is truly alive. Consequently, the abiding truth and urgency of his divine errand are somewhat diminished.

Sophistication and intellectualism

Sophistication and intellectualism can also hinder response. In an era when technology makes it possible for astronauts to become moonwalkers, when communications satellites follow humanly determined orbits, and when computer chips make vast quantities of data instantly available even in our homes, we find it increasingly difficult to affirm God's involvement in presiding over the universe and in caring quite so much about life on planet earth.

Polite discussion and curious speculation concerning God's essence, attributes, and providence may still be respectable, but with increasing cleverness we manage to shut God out of critical areas of our lives. Recognition that we are primarily divine creatures whose fulfillment must be of divine quality challenges and disturbs our self-sufficiency. We might accept Friedrich Schleiermacher's comments to Germany's early nineteenth century intellectuals as fitting for our time. He said that they had been so busy and successful in making themselves comfortable in this world that the idea of God had been fattened out of them. Sophistication and intellectualism have the power to mesmerize us.

Mysticism

Another hindrance is fascination for and reliance on mysticism. This enchantment takes on many forms and expressions. Wesley examined its more classical expressions in sainthood, monasticism, and scholasticism. He reached two conclusions: these forms of seeking union with God are (1) only for certain persons (they cannot be universally imposed), which cancels their usefulness in advancing evangelical Christianity which insists that God's redemption is to be made available to all persons; and (2) little more than forms of self-salvation, salvation by works. Wesley likened such pursuits, however sincere, to his own unproductive efforts to please God and become reunited with the divine. He worked at this task for thirteen years. During that period he did all he could to separate himself from all evil and to have a clear conscience. He made careful and full use of his time. He seized every opportunity for doing good to all persons. He constantly and carefully used all public and private means to worship God and undertake spiritual disciplines. He endeavored to be discreet about his behavior at all times and in all places. He did all this in sincerity. His sole purpose was to serve God. His chief desire was to do God's will in all things. Wesley wanted above all else to please him

who had called him to "fight the good fight" and to "lay hold on
eternal life." In spite of all these efforts he felt himself to be only
"almost a Christian."

In our lifetime we have witnessed a wide variety of so-called
spiritualistic appeals. Some of them border on the exotic. Most of
them revolve around some person who insists that he or she has
special access to divine knowledge and guidance. One by one these
appeals fade. The revitalization of "mainline" denominations has
emerged as a heartening development. Still, we need to keep asking:
Are we championing ethical and moral dimensions that counter
attempts to secularize the gospel? Are we proclaiming as convinc-
ingly as we should the personal benefits and enrichments the good
news promises? Any forms of Christianity that were compromises or
accommodations and that opened up conformity with the world drew
the disdain of Wesley and should draw the same response from us.

Erosion of a critical linkage

Yet another hindrance is what Albert Outler described as "the swift
erosion of the old linkage between anxiety and guilt." We now face
the difficult task of addressing the gospel to those who look upon
themselves as guiltless. Outler described them as "no longer contrite
but . . . still nonetheless hopeless." He cited Richard Niebuhr's concern that the gospel isn't the gospel anymore because we now speak
of "a God without wrath who brought men without sin into a
kingdom without judgment through the ministrations of a Christ
without a Cross."

We want to hear that our sins are merely correctable mistakes or
unfortunate errors of judgment or harmless acts encouraged and
sanctioned by our peers. We compliment the preachers who make us
laugh, but who rarely or never make us weep for our sinfulness. Our
happy-go-lucky society has built an almost impenetrable wall against
believing there is any need at all to think in redemptive terms.

Emotion in religion?

Another consideration hinders the redemptive act. Human beings
seem to have become deathly afraid of any activity that may intro-

duce emotion into religion. Of course, ball games, wrestling matches, movies, political conventions, some books and magazines—all these kinds of events and appeals are fair game for stirring the emotions. Yet the prevailing mood about religious experience is that it should be tempered, even when persons alienated from their heavenly Father for years and years make an about-face and start walking down the dusty road to his house and into his arms!

In examining John Wesley's *Journal* and other writings, George Croft Cell concluded that the founder of Methodism did not particularly encourage violent conversions, but neither did he have a prejudice against them. His consistent teaching was that God works in different ways and that there is great variety in Christian experience. Moreover, there is no evidence that John Wesley himself ever showed marked emotional excitement. He did put on record that his experience of trusting Christ, Christ alone, for his salvation caused his heart to be "strangely warmed."

Perhaps we need to say clearly what has always been true. God suits the emotion to the individual. Those whose lives have been lived out in quietness would find an emotional upheaval out of character, but those whose emotions have always accompanied various kinds of experiences and changed relationships may find that emotion naturally confirms the working of "an inward and spiritual grace."

New challenges in making evangelistic appeals

The phenomenal progress in medical science in extending life expectancy may be a factor in developing new justifications for making evangelical appeals. Longer life spans should make us eager for more opportunities to witness instead of more time merely "to think about it." A pastor is no longer cast in the role of "a dying man speaking to dying men." Our wilderness circuit-riding pioneers had an average life expectancy of less than thirty years. All that has changed. Many persons now believe that delayed commitment to God will not be disastrous. They argue that there is plenty of time before we must come to grips with the question of personal redemption.

A problem faced by early Methodism may be more serious now than it was then: the real and only issue is not whether instantaneous conversion is necessary, but whether any kind of conversion is necessary.

Election and predestination

The twin doctrines of election and predestination may paralyze a response. I have never met anyone yet who believed in these doctrines and felt that he or she was not among the elect! Wesley cut into these scriptural misinterpretations sharply. He held that the doctrine of election made preaching unnecessary. The "elect" didn't need it because, with or without preaching, they would be saved anyway. Since the purpose of preaching is to save souls, he argued, the elect would not regard themselves as being in jeopardy or in need. Those not elected would find no value in hearing sermons because they could not possibly be saved.

Wesley went so far as to say that the doctrine of predestination represented Christ as a hypocrite. In proclaiming the good news, Jesus let persons know that it was God's will for them that they should all be saved. God would be less than a caring God if some people were simply foredoomed—but that implication can rightly be inferred from the doctrine of predestination. God is not in the business of dealing cruelly with people. Those who are separated from God decide this for themselves. Whoever does not truly love God would find even heaven to be hell.

The list of hindrances could go on and on. It takes imagination, patience, and courage to win victories that reconcile an alienated people with their God. But the need for experiential confirmation of the restored human-God relationship is critical and fundamental, so much so that Wesley, based on his own experience, felt that unless the highest truth-values of the gospel are known experientially and practically, they will never be known at all.

We turn now to the overtures God has made to encourage us to attempt the bold task of spiritual recovery.

CHAPTER TWO

GOD'S OVERTURES TO EFFECT RESTORATION

he grand surprise in the salvation drama is the generosity of God. God is the one who was offended and grieved by human arrogance, yet has made remarkable overtures to encourage our restoration. As a moral God, he cannot compel the reconciliation because that would violate the God-given human right to exercise real choice. Besides that, forced fellowship would not result in true fellowship.

PREVENIENT GRACE

God invests our lives with discontent. We are restless until we rest in him. We do everything imaginable to assert our independence, but we cannot remove from the nature of our being the fact that we are unlike any other creature. The discontent that constantly tugs at us is God-given, it is God's grace at work in us. Bishop Ralph S. Cushman wrote some verses that speak to this condition.

> I have heard it in the mountains,
>   I have heard it by the sea,
> Where the plains are vast, and vaster,
> I have heard it calling, calling,
>   Ever calling unto me!
>
> In the nighttime I have heard it
>   Through the darkness and the gloom,
> In the morning when the sunrise
>   Bursts in splendor through my room.

11

Oh, what is it that is calling
In the mountains, by the sea,
In the nighttime, in the daytime,
Ever calling unto me?

Oh, my soul, and can it be
It is God, and He is calling,
Ever calling, calling, calling,
Ever calling unto me?*

But more than discontent is imbedded in our nature. Can any of us remember the first time in our lives when we wished to please God? Perhaps it was when we recited the simple childhood prayer: "And make me a good boy (or girl)." Or there may have been a glimmer of light when we were challenged to make a commitment we thought was beyond our ability. Or something "inside" told us when we did something wrong or said something inappropriate.

In all these ways and more God's grace has been working in us, even without our acknowledging God as the source. God who "keeps on loving us still," works quietly and patiently with us. The word Wesley used to describe this divine activity was *prevenient* or *preventing* grace. It is a gentle love that will not let us go. Even though we have abandoned God, God has not abandoned us.

CONVINCING GRACE

God has made another overture to encourage and effect our restoration. Wesley called it *convincing grace*. Following the lead of conscience, our lives become exposed to divine expectations and we enter the stage of repentance. We acknowledge our utter sinfulness, guilt, and helplessness. Repentance itself does not bring us back into a fully restored relationship. It does, however, make us receptive to God's next overture—saving grace.

SAVING GRACE

Saint Paul, in plain language, described *saving grace* in Ephesians 2:8 in these familiar words: "By grace you have been saved through

*From *A Pocket Prayer Book and Devotional Guide*, compiled by Ralph S. Cushman. Copyright renewed 1969. Used by permission of Upper Room Books.

faith; and this is not your own doing, it is the gift of God—not because of works, lest any man should boast." Because this is the most critical moment in the restoration drama, God has provided special help. At great risk God condescended to reveal God's glory to us by sending Jesus Christ into the world. Through his brief life on earth and by his sacrificial death, Jesus Christ revealed God to us in ways never before known. So completely did he reveal the glory of God that we have come to realize that if we want to know what God is like, we can look at Jesus Christ and see.

He was distinguished for his absolute purity, by his serving faithfully as God's channel for mercy, and by "his death upon the cross for our redemption" (as the Lord's Supper ritual always reminds us). It saddens us that his cruel death came on the insistence of the "religious" community in unholy alliance with pagan powers. But that event brought into clear view the fact that God was willing to risk heartbreak to let us know how much we are loved and how far God will go to make restoration possible. God proved the divine intention by giving evil its ultimate opportunity to do its cruel worst against him. And the children of evil did just that by reducing the beloved Son to mockery and cruel suffering. But God made swift mockery of evil, demonstrating divine power by raising Christ in triumph over sin, death, and the grave.

So when Paul answered the frightened Philippian jailer's question, "What must I do to be saved?" he could put into a single sentence the simple, irrefutable answer: "Believe in the Lord Jesus, and you will be saved" (Acts 16:31). Wesley came to the same conclusion, writing that the key to his heartwarming experience was that he felt he did trust in Christ alone for salvation. He received assurance that Christ had taken away his sins and saved him from both sin and death. Under the evangelical influences that flowed from Wesley's life and work, many persons came under the same power. The transformation of John Newton, who wrote "Amazing Grace," is one remarkable example. Once a trader of slaves then, after his conversion, a minister to them, the epitaph of his London tombstone reads, in part:

John Newton, Clerk
Once an infidel and libertine
And Servant of slaves in Africa
Was by the rich mercy of our Lord and Saviour

> Jesus Christ
> Preserved, restored, pardoned
> And appointed to preach the Faith
> He had labored long to destroy.

JUSTIFICATION BY FAITH ALONE

The doctrine of justification by faith alone embraces preventing, convincing, and saving grace. When Wesley reflected on the significance of this doctrine, he admitted that he regarded it as theological novelty before he gave Christ lordship over his life in 1738. Many others in the Church of England shared that view. That similarity is not surprising, considering the fact that moral rectitude rather than divine grace was the prevailing Anglican view of salvation. Interpreted in this way, Christianity was the belief that human beings sinned only by choice. The Christian life, therefore, emphasized moral effort that was encouraged, sanctioned, and rewarded by the church.

By the end of 1738, Wesley had made a decisive switch from the prevailing notion of self-achieved moral righteousness to justification by faith alone. His thinking moved away from any dependence at all on human merit. Radical trust in God's pardon as a gift, in and through Christ's mediating sacrifice—that was the gospel! Wesley became convinced that he was not only delivered from the guilt of sin but he was restored to the favor of God.

Once Charles Wesley had experienced this God-given victory (shortly before his brother John's Aldersgate experience), he could write the lines of "And Can It Be That I Should Gain":

> Long my imprisoned spirit lay,
> Fast bound in sin and nature's night;
> Thine eye diffused a quickening ray;
> I woke, the dungeon flamed with light;
> My chains fell off, my heart was free,
> I rose, went forth, and followed Thee.
>
> *The United Methodist Hymnal,* 363

We may have the feeling that this reconciliation is no longer being experienced. Let me share a letter my wife and I received from our daughter November 4, 1971. From childhood, Deborah Jean was active in the church. On a family trip to the Middle East when she was fifteen years old, she showed keen interest in the sacred places of the Holy Land. At the time she wrote the letter she was a schoolteacher working with ninth graders, many of whom were from limited family circumstances. She was enjoying life to the full. But she longed for some larger meaning. God led her into such an experience. This is what her letter said.

This has been a very, very special day in my life. I feel as though it's almost impossible to express it in words. [In the next paragraph she told about having an unusually difficult day with her classes of teenagers. Then the letter continued:]

On top of all this, I started thinking about my future and my ultimate purpose and plans. I kept thinking, I'm not even sure what kind of life I want. I just felt very small, insignificant, alone.

But I knew that I just had to go to church [her church was in a weeklong spiritual development series]. In our small group we talked about "Taking a Look at Ourselves." It seemed that everything that was said was in answer to my problem. It just kept building up. I had this strange feeling that something very wonderful was happening to me. The whole time I sat there I kept having this feeling that God was really, really there, right with me. Not only that, but He even seemed to stand with me and go back to my pew after I went forward for prayer.

I know that I have always been a Christian and never doubted that there was a God. But he always seemed to be just a step away, and it was I who just couldn't take that step. But tonight, without even realizing it, I must have taken that step I have been wanting to take for many years.

Tonight I truly realized that the "amazing grace" is something real. I've never felt so completely taken in by the loving God who is so alive in our world.

I feel as though I am a completely different person. I don't think that it was so much a matter of being forgiven of all my sins (although I know I am not guiltless) as it was the realization that God really cares about what happens to me, right now, this minute, tomorrow, and for all the days of my life. He cares what happens when I walk in my class tomorrow. He cares about who I will marry and what kind of home I have. I feel so elated, so relieved, so full of joy.

I want to say that your love of God, for each other, for your children guided me all the way to that last step that I had to take on my own.

The bestowal of this glorious gift upon us by our everloving God is nothing less than a watershed experience. It divides the years of our lives into what we were *before* the experience and what we become *after* the experience. We are no longer forlorn or wayward, but accepted and loyal. It is little wonder that Jesus called it being "born anew."

CONTINUING GRACE

God's grace has yet another role to play in order to protect our restoration from possible failure. Just as a newborn needs constant attention and care from concerned adults, so also does the newborn child of the spirit require spiritual nurture. We can describe this as the work of God's *continuing grace*. It is primarily mediated by the Holy Spirit—God's constant, encouraging presence in our lives.

In his final hours with his disciples, Jesus spoke again and again about the help they would receive from the Holy Spirit:

I will pray the Father, and he will give you another Counselor, to be with you for ever, even the Spirit of truth, whom the world cannot receive, because it neither sees him nor knows him; you know him, for he dwells with you, and will be in you (John 14:16-17).

The Counselor, the Holy Spirit, whom the Father will send in my name, he will teach you all things, and bring to your remembrance all that I have said to you (verse 26).

When the Counselor comes, whom I shall send to you from the Father, even the Spirit of truth, who proceeds from the Father, he will bear witness to me (15:26).

It is to your advantage that I go away, for if I do not go away, the Counselor will not come to you; but if I go, I will send him to you.

And when he comes, he will convince the world of sin and of righteousness and of judgment (16:7-8).

When the Spirit of truth comes, he will guide you into all the truth (verse 13).

When we welcome the Holy Spirit into our lives, as the disciples did so long ago, our day-by-day experiences are governed by a disposition that Wesley called "scriptural holiness" or sanctification. This constant divine control of our spirit deflects the power of sin. The holy God, and we as reconciled children who eagerly desire the Holy Spirit to nurture both inward and outward holiness, now become mutually involved in a relationship of peace and joy. When sanctification can be embraced as the natural temperament of those who are reconciled to their Creator, then the Moravian description of the fully redeemed life can be understood. The interplay of God's grace and our glad response is assuring, heartwarming, liberating, regenerating, and full of cleansing and uplifting power.

Wesley fostered a sensible approach to sanctification. He believed sanctification to be inward. He thought of it as the life of God in the soul of human beings, participation of the divine nature in the human spirit, letting the mind that was in Christ be also in us. Sanctification affirms that our hearts are renewed after the image of our Creator-God. Wesley's illustration of what this renewal means, found in *A Plain Account of Christian Perfection,* is so applicable and true: A very little dust will disorder a clock, he wrote, and the least sand will obscure our sight. In much the same way, he concluded, the least grain of sin that is upon the heart will hinder its right motion toward God.

Martin Luther also encouraged Christians who wanted to pursue the spiritual renewal of the soul. He spoke of faith as God's work in us. Faith makes us utterly different in heart, disposition, spirit, and in all our faculties. The Holy Spirit is dynamically present in all of these changes. Something vital, busy, active, and powerful makes us more and more joyful in pursuing good works. This lively, reckless confidence in the grace of God can make us buoyant, more sure of ourselves, bold-hearted, and content toward God and all creation. This was Luther's Christian lifestyle.

The closing portion of the Wesleyan Covenant Service provides a good description of the sanctified person:

I am no longer my own, but thine. Put me to what thou wilt, rank me with whom thou wilt; put me to doing, put me to suffering; let me be employed for thee or laid aside for thee, exalted for thee or brought low for thee; let me be full, let me be empty; let me have all things, let me have nothing; I freely and heartily yield all things to thy pleasure and disposal. And now, O glorious and blessed God, Father, Son, and Holy Spirit, thou art mine, and I am thine. So be it. And the covenant which I have made on earth, let it be ratified in heaven.

The Book of Worship, p. 387

CHAPTER THREE

ALLIES OF FAITH

hen someone asked Thomas Edison, "Don't you think most discoveries are accidental?" the great inventor replied: "It's my observation that discovery favors the trained mind." When we think about persuasive persons who have advanced the Christian faith, we recognize that many of them excelled in disciplining the intellect: Saul of Tarsus was a graduate of the School of Gamaliel; Saint Augustine studied rhetoric at Carthage; Martin Luther earned a Master's Degree at the University of Erfurt; John Wesley became an Oxford don. All these persons ultimately reduced the Christian faith to unmistakably clear fundamentals—the accomplishments of well-honed minds. When the German theologian and church historian Adolph Harnack assessed the great reform movements of Christianity, he concluded they were all marked by a return to simplicity in theology.

THE TRAINED MIND

Methodism has always been on the side of the trained mind. Wesley insisted on "intelligent industry" on the part of his lay preachers. Much of his writing and publishing was for them. In his will he designated that his books be distributed among them. Regarding theological considerations he fixed the limit at the point where any doctrinal formulation ceased to be biblical, experiential, and practical. He rejected severely prescribed theology that was thrust upon the people by the church. His wide-ranging reading is illustrated by the mention in his *Journal* of more than 230 authors of multiple interests.

Because Wesley was so well informed, his critical insights continue to have relevance. In his own time he exposed a kind of humanism, of the intellectualist, the legalist and the mystical kind, which taught people to expect to meet God through their own efforts. His own experience of Christian faith, however, revolutionized all that. The prophetic-Christian message puts the divine initiative first. One of Wesley's favorite and often repeated scripture verses was, "We love, because he first loved us" (1 John 4:19).

Wesley used diverse resources to substantiate his thought. His extensive writings show that he developed wide acquaintance with the general stream of Christian thought. His knowledge and appreciation of historic Christianity helped him develop perspective. One of my seminary teachers was Gaius Jackson Slosser, who taught church history as rigorously as it could be taught. For me his most memorable comment was: "You must understand the church is still in its infancy."

The Church of England, into whose priesthood Wesley was admitted in 1725, troubled him in large part because of its strong leaning toward humanism. This became a deep concern for Wesley by the spring of 1738. By that time he had been exposed to the Noncomformists, who were disenchanted by the established church because of its secularized theology. He found himself becoming sympathetic toward the Noncomformists.

Wesley had read and reread Thomas à Kempis' classic *The Imitation of Christ.* He felt deeply the importance of holiness. By 1738 he had begun to wonder about the effectiveness of withdrawal from the world as the way to achieve the sanctified life. Wesley immersed himself in Luther's writings, and from that source he became convinced that an infinite gulf separated human efforts and God's grace. He believed human beings had to abandon self-salvation and humbly accept the fact that only God could accomplish redemption.

As time went on, Wesley came to the same conclusion Luther did in decrying scholastic theology (including humanistic mysticism), of which he had developed considerable knowledge. He came to look upon scholastic theology as superficial and of no practical value, because it isolated one's religious consciousness from the free, earnest, and active use of the intellect. He attempted to synthesize the Luther-Calvin idea of the sovereign saving significance of a God-given faith in Christ with the English interpretation of Arminianism, which emphasized human response in the salvation process. In Wesley's thinking there was no final contradiction between the human response to grace, and the Calvinist conception of original sin and justification by faith. This was a hard-won intellectual victory for Wesley, since it meant being called a "dissenter" by his Anglican contemporaries, and a "papist" by his Calvinist friends. But he refused to succumb to the power of labels.

At the fourth annual conference of his preachers in 1747, expressing his insistence on the right to think freely about theology, Wesley proclaimed: "Every man must think for himself, since every man must give an account of himself to God." The mind cannot be surrendered to external authority. This position became the first principle of the Enlightenment. It echoed the declarations of Melancthon at Wittenberg in 1520: "Have the courage of your own insight!" and of Luther at about the same time: "Let us dare to think for ourselves!"

The truth we seek from all possible reliable sources must be confirmed by the experience of God in our own lives. This was Wesley's conviction. He was convinced that religious truths can be clearly known only by those who derive knowledge not from commentaries, but from experience. The end result was an inward, practical, experimental, and affective knowledge of God.

REASON

Although our United Methodist tradition places high value on the intellect, it also expects us to guard against relying too heavily on reason to produce spiritual maturity. Wesley knew that reason provided certain benefits—new or refined ideas about faith, life, and love—but reasoning about such matters is not enough. He tried to find satisfaction by feeding his intellect. He collected the finest hymns, prayers, and meditations he could find in any language. He sang, said, or read them over and over, with all possible seriousness and attention. The experiment failed. Thereupon Wesley concluded that reason, when it has done all that it can do, is utterly incapable of producing faith, hope, or love. These must be sought and received solely as gifts of God. God alone can give saving faith.

Wesley, given his inquiring and informed mind, may have believed at one time that he could reason himself through to the Christian faith, but he moved away from that position because it was unproductive. Perhaps recalling the logic he taught at Oxford, he finally concluded that in spite of all his logic he could not prove anything in philosophy or divinity absolutely. He also discovered that the contrast between Saint Paul's failures at Athens and his successes at nearby Corinth were caused by a disconcerting realization. The apostle realized that philosophical and intellectual religion may stir spirited debate, but the message of Jesus Christ the crucified, who never indulged in philosophical or mystical modes of thought, demonstrated spirit and power.

REASON AND FAITH IN ALLIANCE

So what expectations can we hold for using the intellect and reason in understanding and interpreting Christian experience? How can reason be made an ally of faith?

Efforts to elevate humanistic Christianity have depended almost solely on human reason. But Wesley countered humanistic Christianity's claims of sufficiency on the grounds that the mind alone cannot possibly comprehend all that is available from God. Nor can mere intellectual assent to Christian principles of thought and life effect a fundamental transformation of the alienated human spirit.

Two of Wesley's sermons—"The Imperfection of Human Knowledge" and "The Case of Reason Impartially Considered"—deal with this problem. In both sermons he makes the case for intellect. He believed that God would not have given human beings a hunger for knowledge and the power to think through particular questions and issues unless the human mind could deal with primary matters (which, for Wesley, were matters of religion). He believed that God wanted us to use this power "for excellent ends" and regarded reason as a "candle of the Lord."

But the distance between what we know and what God knows, what we are and what God is, will always be infinite. So Wesley conceded that the role of reason should not be disparaged, but neither should its importance be exaggerated. The balance struck by Wesley makes sense. He perceived that religion is designed to perfect the reason or understanding God has given to us. One critic wrote to Wesley, somewhat cynically: "You are for reason, I am for faith." Wesley replied simply, "I am for both."

In urging piety, Wesley had no sympathy for ignorance. He championed religion and reason as allies and declared that irrational religion is false religion. Nevertheless, for Wesley, the final test of reason was not the power of language or logic per se, but the power of God's Spirit and image in the human soul, to love as God loves.

FREE MORAL AGENTS

The delicate balance between reason and faith helps us function effectively as free moral agents. Reason helps us define our highest possible choice. We can realistically regard sin as bondage. We can mount no solid defense for attempting to effect divine restoration by mere wisdom or heroism or freedom. Wesley warned of the danger of overreaching intelligence, saying that it turns into intellectual arrogance.

The grandest of all choices—to let divine grace transform us totally—yields magnificent blessings. Wesley carefully observed that God's grace does not take away our understanding; rather, it enlightens and strengthens it. Grace does not destroy our affections; rather, they become more refined and vigorous. Grace does not take away our liberty, our power of choosing good or evil. God does not force us but, being assisted by God's grace, we can choose the better part without depriving ourselves of that liberty which is an indispensable quality of moral life.

However short we may fall of loving God with all our heart, all our soul, and all our mind, we are privileged to open our hearts, souls, and minds to all that God wants to pour into our lives. When that happens, we reach a high level of spiritual ecstasy. The late Albert E. Day must have had that in mind when he said that the question is not, "What do I have to get rid of to become a Christian?" but rather, "How much of God can I possess?"

Spiritual exhilaration really begins when we move from faith to trust. William A. Smart made that distinction when he told the story of a person standing on a pier watching a great ocean liner getting readied for a transoceanic voyage. He watched the loading of the fuel and supplies. Someone asked, "Do you believe that ship will make the crossing?" "Yes," he answered. Then he presented his ticket, mounted the gangplank, and became an on-board passenger. "That," remarked

Smart, "was the decision that moved him beyond faith and belief to trust."

EXPERIENCE

Reason leads us to the threshold of personal redemptive experience. At that point faith and trust take over. Not according to your reason but "according to your faith be it done to you" said Jesus to two blind men who asked him to restore their sight. Reason brought them into his presence. Then, on his command, faith took charge and "their eyes were opened" (Matthew 9:27-30).

Science announces no conclusions until a sufficient number of experiments provide verification. The United Methodist doctrine of Christian experience is very much like that. The truth-value of religion is confirmed by each individual's experience of its reality. This idea is central to evangelical Christianity. Wesley put every issue of the Christian faith to the test of experimental practice and exposed the verification of every question of theology to applied Christianity.

Before the Reformation the doctrinal question always was: What is the faith of the visible church? Early Protestantism asked: What is the revelation of the Bible? Wesley's contemporaries began to ask: What is religion within the limits of reason alone? Wesley never asked any of those questions. Experience and its indications became for him the citadel of the Christian apologetic.

Wesley forged a connection between experience and scripture, saying that knowledge of the plain teaching of scripture by itself is not enough. The additional credential needed to demonstrate its truth-value was the sure testimony of experience. In his later years he joined scripture and experience more closely and deliberately as mutually connected and complementary for spiritual growth and development. He thought of scripture as the most decisive of all proofs, and of experience as the strongest of all arguments. This realism puts this doctrine clearly in the category of practical theology. It saves believers from emotional excess, on the one hand, and from bibliolatry on the other.

REVELATION

The third significant contribution to vital and vibrant Christian faith (reason and experience being the first two) is revelation. Under Wesleyan doctrine, reason counts for something, experience more, and revelation most. The Wesleyan Movement had to be reckoned with because it gave large place for the involvement of God's own presence by the Spirit of Christ. The dynamic thrust of the Wesleyan Reformation did not come out of any humanistic reconstruction of the Christian faith. The Wesleyan Reformation arose primarily as a powerful reaction against a naturalistic and humanistic reconstruction of Christianity.

During the eighteenth century in England, Christians once again became vibrant. From Wesley to the least conspicuous participant in that movement, spiritually reborn men and women were caught up in joyful Christianity. As human beings they witnessed and participated in the presence of the transcendent God in the world as the immanent God. The results were exhilarating. Wesley was right on track when he said that the first source and mainspring of the Christian consciousness is to think of God as far superior to this present good and evil world. God is much better than our best; God is more excellent than our highest knowledge, thought, or experience.

Each new generation must ask the timeless question: How can Christians receive and cooperate with God's presence in the world, altering the dismal human condition? The writer of First Peter gives us an assignment: "Always be prepared to make a defense to any one who calls you to account for the hope that is in you, yet do it with gentleness and reverence" (1 Peter 3:15).

CHAPTER FOUR

TRANSFORMATIONS

he experience that restores a person to God's affection inevitably transforms our relationships with one another. We belong to God and the world in new ways. When our hearts turn away from ourselves (the creature) to God (the Creator), an almost immediate dispositional change occurs. In contrast to our previous superficial happiness, a new and unspeakable joy begins to become real and substantial.

We now belong to God by God's grace and by our choice. We comprehend the paradox in George Matheson's hymn:

> Make me a captive, Lord,
> And then I shall be free
>
> . . . .
>
> Imprison me within thine arms,
> And strong shall be my hand
>
> . . . .
>
> My will is not my own
> Till thou hast made it thine.
>
> *The United Methodist Hymnal, 421*

Even prayer takes on new meaning and importance as it serves not so much to seek divine favor, but to enliven and deepen the consciousness of our continued and total reliance on God.

Family life also takes on new meaning and obligation. Bishop Francis J. McConnell placed alongside Methodism's emphases on conversion, sanctification, and assurance the religious training of children. He made the point that the child born in a Christian home is marked from birth for the kingdom of God. He reminded Christians that a human being is entitled to and can respond to divine influences from infancy. He added that the growing child's later spiritual experiences are made possible as he or she is drawn close to the church and a caring family. The bishop knew, of course, that a child born into a Christian home might conceivably never commit gross sin. Yet he or she must ratify the mode of life received through the influence of godly parents. We can hardly read Luke 2:41-51 without thinking that the encounter between the boy Jesus and the Hebrew teachers in the Temple marked a turning-point in his life. There ought to come a time when every child is given the opportunity to make a decision or take a stand in ratification of the truth he or she has been taught.

But Methodism, along with other evangelically minded denominations, would not exclude children who are not exposed to a Christian family environment from admittance into the family of God. One phrase included in the ritual for the baptism of children is especially appropriate. When that sacrament is administered, the child is recognized as "a member of the family of God."

In my beginning ministry, while serving a congregation in an underprivileged area of a large city, I received an invitation to administer the sacrament of baptism in an unusual circumstance. Here is the story.

They were a very young couple, probably in their mid-teens. An elderly woman who lived in the narrow alley where they also lived discovered them. This elderly woman, a member of the church, was always taking me, her pastor, to help needy families. One night after our midweek service, she said: "Pastor, bring your little black book and come with me."

We walked down the dark alley a block or so from the church. We climbed the rickety steps of a dilapidated building. She rapped gently on the door. A gaunt young man greeted us. "I brought him," my friend said as she nudged me inside.

A fifteen-watt light bulb provided the only illumination in the room. After my eyes adjusted to the dimly lit surroundings, I saw a wisp of a girl bending over an improvised crib. "This is my wife," the young man said. "She wanted you to come."

She looked up and said, "This is our baby. Please tell me if you think she is going to die."

I stepped over to the cradle and touched the hot forehead of the sleeping infant. "I am young like you," I said, "and I don't know much about such things, but I do know that your little girl is very sick."

"But is she going to die?" the young mother asked again.

"I can't answer that question," I replied.

Then the father spoke: "I don't know what it means, because we aren't church folks, but we would feel better if you would baptize her."

I asked them to put some water in a dish. The frail mother found a chipped bowl in a closet and filled it with water from the single faucet at the sink. I read the ritual for the baptism of infants, took the feverish child in my arms, and baptized her into "the family of God."

The anxious parents clung to each other. Their little neighbor from the alley stood by quietly. I laid the child back in the crib and drew the tattered coverlet over her. Then we joined hands—the parents, the neighbor, and I—and prayed together. As I left I promised them I would return if they called for me.

Two days later the call came. The child had died. I spent two days gathering up money to buy a burial plot and persuaded the funeral director to provide a small casket without cost. Then we commended her into God's eternal care and keeping.

That encounter early in my life with a frightened little family introduced me to a world I had never seen before. But it is a world our heavenly Parent gazes upon all the time. God's grace extends to all people, including little helpless children. While the fullest description of United Methodist understanding of baptism would also include confirmation, and reaffirmation, these do not cancel the reality of God's grace and kingdom, even in the most modest acts of tender ministration.

Jesus used the phrases "kingdom of heaven" and "kingdom of God" interchangeably. We know he encouraged his disciples to pray: "Thy kingdom come, thy will be done, on earth as it is in heaven." This is the very first petition of the Lord's Prayer. A future, happy, eternal state will follow the state we now enjoy here on earth. Those who tell us they experience the kingdom of God within themselves every day are putting this present world in appropriate spiritual perspective.

Some persons speak of Wesley as having been austere, but he was quite the opposite. There is ample evidence to believe that he was a truly joyous and spirited man. How else could he have declared in his sermon, "The Way to the Kingdom": "Glory is on earth begun . . . Where Thy presence is displayed, 'tis heaven" (John Wesley, *Sermons on Several Occasions*, pp. 78-79). He enjoyed what Ralph Sockman called "the higher happiness," defining the kingdom of glory in heaven as the continuation and perfection of the kingdom of grace on earth.

This kingdom is just as real as (and, for Christians, more important than) any other kingdom with which we may be identified. Bishop McConnell spoke about kingdoms of learning, patriotism, and art, observing that persons reach these kingdoms as they respond to the powers and influences that direct these kingdoms. In much the same way, we become citizens of the kingdom of the Spirit.

Citizenship in this kingdom is our primary citizenship. Interestingly, this membership is evidenced in a regulation in United States military procedure. The only emblem permitted to fly above the American flag is the emblem of the cross, and this is prescribed to be done only during community, army, navy, or congregational prayer and in the midst of devotional service. Every battleship carries the Christian flag, and regulation requires that this "white pennant with blue cross" float above the Stars and Stripes for one hour every Sunday—and be placed at stern. The navy and marine bands at this function play "Onward, Christian Soldiers" and close the service with the National Anthem.

In the mid-nineteenth century Great Britain ruled the world. The most powerful person of that era was Queen Victoria. You may know the story associated with her beginning years as reigning monarch. When she had just ascended the throne, she went, as is the custom of British royalty, to hear a rendering of Handel's incomparable oratorio, "The Messiah." She had been instructed as to her conduct by those who knew. She was told she must not stand when the others stood at the singing of the "Hallelujah Chorus."

The magnificent finale was being sung at full volume: "Hallelujah! Hallelujah! Hallelujah! for the Lord God omnipotent reigneth." She remained seated with great difficulty. It seemed as if she would rise in spite of the custom of kings and queens. Finally they came to that part of the chorus where with a shout they proclaimed Christ "King of kings and Lord of lords." The young queen suddenly rose to her feet and bowed her head.

On August 17, 1758, John Wesley went to hear the same oratorio at Saint Paul's Cathedral and recorded in his *Journal:* "I doubt if that congregation was ever so serious at a sermon, as they were during this performance. In many parts, especially several of the choruses, it exceeded my expectations" (Thomas Jackson, ed., *The Works of John Wesley,* Vol. II, P. 456).

Many paraphrased editions (they could hardly be regarded as translations) of the Bible are coming into circulation nowadays, some of doubtful scholarship. One disturbing comment I hear is that, in order to eliminate sexist language and "male dominance," one version may be produced that will drop the words *king* and *lord* with reference to Christ. This biblical characterization of Jesus fittingly ascribes to him the recognition of the highest royalty—divine royalty. Over the kingdom of God, he is the king; for us as citizens of the kingdom of God, he is lord.

THE CHRISTIAN'S DUAL CITIZENSHIP

Our dual citizenship makes us grateful to think of this present earthbound kingdom as "my Father's world." Yet we realize every day that our reconciliation to God makes us children in the Spirit, enabling us to look with some detachment upon any and all kingdoms of this present world.

This idea was impressed on me when I worshiped with a Christian congregation in Canton, China. After the service I asked the pastor if he had any difficulty in having the Chinese national flag placed alongside the Christian flag in the chancel. "Do you place the American flag in your churches?" he asked. "Yes," I said. "Does that mean that you agree with everything your government does?" "No," I replied. "Well," he said, "just as being a Christian doesn't make you less an American, being a Christian doesn't make me less a Chinese." The argument was irrefutable. Yet for all Christians, under whatever national allegiance they fulfill their earthly citizenship, there is a kind of holy detachment because we all know that ultimately, as Revelation 11:15 so magnificently proclaims, "The kingdoms of this world are become the kingdoms of our Lord, and of his Christ; and he shall reign for ever and ever" (KJV).

We qualify for citizenship in the kingdom of God when we are molded into Christlikeness. Wesley discovered that the Son of God strikes at the root of pride, at the root of self-will. He destroys the love of the world, delivering those who believe in him from the "desire of the flesh, the desire of the eyes, and the pride of life" (1 John 2:16). Our new and chief employment on earth, as those whose primary allegiance is to the higher kingdom, is to work for divine solutions to human problems. We will give attention to that task in the next chapter.

United Methodists recognize certain minimal characteristics of the kingdom of God that represent our tradition faithfully and give us leverage for our own witness. These minimal characteristics would most certainly include the following:

An ecumenical spirit

We have already noticed that Wesley drew freely from a variety of Christian traditions in developing his system of thought. First, he never surrendered his Anglican priesthood and he never encouraged the Methodists in England to leave the established church. He carefully, critically, and sympathetically examined theological perspectives held by Calvin, Luther, the Moravians, Arminius, and Roman Catholicism, acknowledging a debt to all of them as he recast scriptural evangelical faith.

This quite remarkable and distinctive ecumenical spirit that marked the beginning of our United Methodist heritage has given us warrant for continuing cordial relationships with Christians of other-than-United Methodist affiliation. We claim no corner on the kingdom of God, either on earth or in heaven. In most communities we take initiative in developing cooperative witness among all Christians. We open our fellowship to persons of other traditions without requiring special instruction as they reaffirm their faith, nor do we insist on a particular kind of rite or rebaptism for admission to a given congregation. Once a person is recognized by the Body of Christ as a member of the "family of God," we affirm and confirm that recognition without imposing additional requirements.

A spiritual democracy

We have an ongoing tradition of being a denomination that can be described as a spiritual democracy. In many ways, even from our eighteenth-century beginnings, we have given leadership roles to the laity. When Wesley was criticized for developing a program using the services of carefully instructed lay preachers, he answered: "Was Mr. Calvin ordained? Was he either Priest or Deacon? And were not most of those whom it pleased God to employ in promoting the Reformation abroad, laymen also?" (Jackson, ed., *Works,* Vol. VIII, p. 222).

Not only do laypersons share leadership roles with clergy, but the conditions for membership in the church are conditions that anyone who desires can fulfill. The questions, plainly worded, are found in the ritual for reception into church membership: "Do you . . . renew the solemn promise and vow that you made, or that was made in your name, at your Baptism? . . . Do you confess Jesus Christ as your Lord and Savior and pledge your allegiance to his kingdom? Do you . . . receive and profess the Christian faith as contained in the Scriptures of the Old and New Testaments? . . . Do you promise according to the grace given you to live a Christian life and always remain a faithful member of Christ's holy Church? . . . Will you be loyal to The United Methodist Church, and uphold it by your prayers, your presence, your gifts, and your service?" (*The Book of Worship,* pp. 12-13). A more direct, simplified expectation for entering the fellowship could hardly be proposed. The democracy is genuine.

An illustration of this democracy is found in Charles Wesley's hymn "A Charge to Keep I Have." Customarily we use this hymn on occasions when clergy are ordained or when we install laypersons in church offices. The hymn was written for artisans, merchants, and coal miners! It was written to give divine meaning to everyday labor. With that in mind, read again the words of that great hymn, noticing how it can elevate the thinking of common workers to the highest level of Christian dedication:

> A charge to keep I have,
> A God to glorify,
> A never-dying soul to save,
> And fit it for the sky.
>
> To serve the present age,
> My calling to fulfill;
> O may it all my powers engage
> To do my Master's will!

Arm me with jealous care,
  As in thy sight to live,
And oh, thy servant, Lord, prepare
  A strict account to give!

Help me to watch and pray,
  And on thyself rely,
Assured, if I my trust betray,
  I shall forever die.

The United Methodist Hymnal, 413

Sometimes we forget the Christian insistence that every person has dignity. It is senseless to put down anyone as being less valuable than ourselves. One Sunday morning I arrived at the church a little early. An irate member met me at the door.

"Where's the janitor?" she asked.

"I don't really know," I replied. "I just got here myself. Is something wrong?"

"Is something *wrong?* Something certainly is wrong. Go in the sanctuary and look at all that dust on the altar."

"Is that all?" I asked. "Do you know where the dust cloths are?"

"Of course, I do. I'm chairman of the Altar Guild."

"Good. Why don't you get a cloth and dust off the altar?"

"Who, me? After all, we pay the janitor to do that."

As I turned to walk away, I ended the conversation by saying, "You know, I've never dusted off the altar of the Lord. Today the custodian's oversight gives me that opportunity. It will be a privilege to go and dust it off as a service to God." That task did not belittle my office as pastor of the church.

I was a little too inexperienced then to know something more important—there is no task too modest for any member of the Body of Christ to perform if God needs it done. That principle is at the heart of our cherished spiritual democracy.

Any time we inflict self-seeking or arrogance on the society of the redeemed, we render great disservice to the kingdom of God. When Wesley interpreted Matthew 16:24, he translated "renounce" as the equivalent of "deny." Look at what that does to that familiar invitation Jesus gave to candidates for discipleship: "If any man would come after me, let him *renounce* himself and take up his cross and follow me." In plain speech that means: "For heaven's sake, get down off the throne and let the Lord sit there!" How well each of us knows that the self is a most obstinate usurper.

A community of mutual helpfulness

United Methodism believes that the kingdom of God introduces us to a community of mutual helpfulness. I like to think that this marvelous characteristic of those who are in the kingdom goes back to that conversation between Jesus and Simon Peter in the upper room. Jesus anticipated Peter's denial, but he looked beyond it and said to him: "Simon, Simon, behold, Satan demanded to have you, that he might sift you like wheat, but I have prayed for you that your faith may not fail; and *when you have turned again, strengthen your brethren*" (Luke 22:31-32). This obligation becomes the vocation of everyone who enters the kingdom of God.

Near the end of the year 1739, eight or ten persons visited John Wesley in London. They wanted him to spend time with them in prayer and advise them on how to flee from the wrath to come. Wesley was grateful for their errand and appreciated their request. He believed that they and others should have more opportunity for this work. So he appointed a time when they might all come together— every Thursday in the evening. This marked the beginning of the United Society, first in London, and then in other places. Wesley described this society as a company of persons having the form and seeking the power of godliness, united in order to pray together, to receive the word of exhortation, and to watch over one another in love, that they may help each other to work out their salvation. What an imaginative idea.

This Wesleyan tradition seems to have fallen on hard times in recent decades (particularly with the demise of the midweek prayer-meeting in most of our churches), but regular opportunities for mutual spiritual helpfulness do enhance the vitality and spiritual integrity of the fellowship.

When I was a boy, I was told that my paternal grandfather kept this Wesleyan tradition alive in his remote rural church in central Pennsylvania. He served as a Class Leader for more than forty years. He could have grown discouraged and even given up, but he never did. One wintry night he walked through deep snow from his log house to the little church three miles away.

When he returned home, my grandmother asked, "How was it tonight? Did you have a good meeting?"

"Yes." he told her, "we had a good meeting."

"How many were there?"

"Two."

"You and who else?"

"God—God and I."

"But what did you do?"

"Well, we read the scripture together and we prayed together. It was a good Class Meeting."

I wouldn't part with that recollection of our family's heritage for anything. It was an affirmation of faithfulness. I wish there were some way to recover this heritage in more families.

Beyond the church

The kingdom of God shows itself when it breaks out into the secular, humanistic world—the kingdom of God beyond the church. When we are attuned to God's reign in our lives, even simple things can take on new meaning. One night in an evangelistic meeting my maternal grandfather renounced himself (to use Wesley's word) and allowed the enthroned Christ to radically alter his view of life around him. The very next morning he went out to the barn to saddle up his horse. With his new life in Christ begun, he looked into the face of his horse and said, "Why, Jim, have you been converted, too?"

Daily routines become for the Christian daily opportunities. More than that, they must be seized upon for God's purposes. Wesley was a careful steward of time. He came to the conclusion that no employment of our time, no action, and no conversation is purely indifferent. Our time is not our own. It belongs to God our Creator. We can use or fail to use this divine gift in fulfilling God's purposes.

Similarly, we might remind ourselves that sanctification can mean very little apart from the social expression of religion. We cannot draw a line between what persons are in themselves and what they are in relation to others. We live and move and have a large part of our being in relation to other persons.

The late Roy L. Smith cultivated a holy imagination. He once suggested a "final chapter" for the unfinished story of the woman taken in adultery. You know the abrupt ending. After all her accusers faded away: "Jesus looked up and said to her, 'Woman, where are they? Has no one condemned you?' She said, 'No one, Lord.' And Jesus said, 'Neither do I condemn you; go, and do not sin again'" (John 8:10-11). Smith latched onto that phrase, "do not sin again." "What did that mean for her if she obeyed Jesus?" Smith asked. Then he went on to answer his question: "She had to change her vocation, she probably had to move to other living quarters, and she had to find a whole new circle of friends."

As reconciled children of God who comprise the Body of Christ, we are obligated to help the kingdom break through into the world around us. United Methodism keeps calling us to reflect the spirit of Christ at all times, in all places, and in all that we do and say. There may be ways for God to break through without our participation, but there isn't much evidence that anything happens that way.

Release from fear of the future

The last characteristic of the kingdom of God I will mention is that this kingdom extends beyond the years of our flesh. When we are saved from our sin and guilt, we enter the kingdom of God on earth, but God's grace also releases us from fear of the future. Saint Paul used the tenderest of salutations when he addressed God in Romans 8:15-17: "You did not receive the spirit of slavery to fall back into fear, but you have received the spirit of sonship. When we cry, *'Abba! Father!'*, it is the Spirit himself bearing witness with our spirit that we are children of God, and if children, then *heirs,* heirs of God and fellow heirs with Christ, provided we suffer with him in order that we may also be glorified with him." In that same letter Paul affirmed with great confidence the durability of the love between the believer and Christ: "I am sure that neither death, nor life, nor angels, nor principalities, nor things present, nor things to come, nor powers, nor height, nor depth, nor anything else in all creation, will be able to separate us from the love of God in Christ Jesus our Lord" (Romans 8:38-39).

CHAPTER FIVE

THE GOSPEL FOR
THE WORLD

hristians must assess and resolve their relationship to this present world. Jesus' intercessory prayer took that need into account. He prayed for his immediate disciples that they would not be taken out of the world (John 17:15). In fact, he deliberately sent them into the world (verse 18)!

Divine reconciliation changes our perspective on this present world: we are to be in it but not of it. Each of us becomes, as an old song reminded us, "a stranger here within a foreign land. . . . Ambassador to be from realms beyond the sea, I'm here on business for my King."

A reminder of the historical sources of Protestantism is helpful. More than two centuries ago Wesley resisted the drift toward the worship of humanity. With a mighty summons, much like the faith of the European Reformers, he called for a return to the worship of God in the Christian sense. At the center of Wesley's greatness was his determination to consecrate every moment and every faculty of his being to Jesus, and to Jesus' call to love God and neighbor.

Wesley carried on a running battle with those forms of mysticism which ignored the call to seek the kingdom of God in this world. He believed that the notion of the mystics, "the flight of the alone to the Alone," cancelled out Christian realism. At the same time he chided the church for not seeking an adequate answer to the question, What is the church *for* in the world? The experience of Christ within one's heart must be augmented with outward moral and ethical expressions. Christians in the Wesleyan tradition will always carry on a running battle with any self-serving form of salvation.

THE WITNESS OF CHRISTIAN SERVICE

Wesley put strong emphasis on the witness of the Spirit, but his age knew that he put just as much emphasis on the witness of Christian service as the end and sign of active faith. Praying for God's grace and forgiveness is pointless unless it brings forth many kinds of divinely inspired activities. High on the list of such activities would be the love of one's neighbor in service to all humankind, peacemaking, and many other concrete forms of service. We show our love for God in humbleness of life; we show our love for others in generous and joyful service.

The Sermon on the Mount is full of this idea, calling on us to carry the good news to a world that seems to always churn up bad news. Any way we introduce and apply the divine will to our troubled world gives the divine a little more leverage in putting God back into human affairs and into human history.

The Holy Club at Oxford, to which the Wesley brothers belonged, was an object of ridicule by the students there. Holy Club members studied the scriptures diligently, cultivated the life of prayer, and undertook other personal spiritual exercises. This little group of young men set aside blocks of time every day to serve the poor, those in prison, and other persons who were experiencing the misery of lovelessness and neglect.

This commitment by Wesley in his early years, even though it was cynically ridiculed by some contemporaries, seemed to grow stronger as he grew older. His social sensitivity came to even more aggressive expression after his heartwarming experience in 1738. His motivation became something more than merely engaging in good works to please God; it became a primary way for sharing the love of God that had dramatically changed him. He was so much involved in activist Christianity that his friend and distinguished man of letters, Samuel Johnson, complained that Wesley never had time to sit down and talk anything through. He was always in a hurry to get on to some practical task. Wesley was as disdainful of sedentary Christianity as of solitary Christianity.

SECRET CHRISTIANITY—A CONTRADICTION

Nor did Wesley have any interest in secret Christianity. The Gospel narrative speaks of Joseph of Arimathea as a secret disciple (John 19:38). Except for his generosity in making a sepulchre available for Jesus' temporary burial, we have no record of his ever espousing, defending, or advancing the new faith.

Wesley insisted on applying Christian principles to all the outward affairs of society. He was convinced that it was impossible for any that claimed to be Christian to conceal their faith. He reminded his friends of the words of Jesus: "You are the light of the world: a city set upon a hill cannot be hid" (Matt. 5:14). The Christian's holiness makes him or her as conspicuous as the sun. Wesley felt that love could not be hidden any more than light. He insisted that secret, unobserved religion could not be the religion of Jesus Christ.

Our task, then, is to let the world beyond the church discover and know the goodness of God. We are obligated and privileged to bring the gospel to bear upon the living, aching concerns of contemporary men and women as they live from day to day.

MISSION AND MISSIONS

United Methodism has been wrestling in recent years with the relationship between mission and missions. What are the functions and responsibilities of the church beyond the church? What doors are open for witness and what doors are now closed? Can we adjust to being *partners* in mission rather than *leaders* in missions?

A missionary who dedicated his years of service in southeast Asia came to the conclusion that his task was to work himself out of a job. He served unselfishly and diligently to bring the people there as quickly as possible to Christian maturity and responsibility, believing that, as natives, their witness for Christ could be more productive than his witness from the West.

When I asked Bishop Deng in Nanking what we Christians in America could do to encourage the Chinese Christians, he responded:

The Methodists have already done much. You were the first mainline denomination in America that, by General Conference resolution, called for reopening United States' relationships with the

People's Republic—and you did that when it was not a popular position. As for the churches, do not send us any missionaries. We have more Christians in China today than we had before the Cultural Revolution and we can now develop our own leadership. And do not send us any Bibles or Testaments from America. We are printing our own and we like the feel of holding the Scriptures in a form which we ourselves produced. What you can do is continue to be our friends in Christ and keep on praying for us.

I was somewhat chagrined when a Chinese pastor told me it was the prayers of the American Christians which sustained the Chinese Christians who were compelled to form "underground" house churches during the incredibly difficult years of the Cultural Revolution. I was chagrined because I had not prayed even once for the Chinese Christians during those years of their ordeal, publicly or privately. Perhaps you did.

THE SPIRIT OF CHRIST AND THE SPIRIT OF THE WORLD

Certainly any assessment of "mission" must recognize the contrast between the spirit of Christ and the spirit of the world, a difference Wesley recognized. The Wesleyan Revival produced a revolution not only in faith but also in morals. The spirit of Christ, wherever it is sown and takes root, affects and alters human thought and conduct. United Methodists are historically committed to human dignity. Christianity, from its New Testament beginnings, has always tried to bless rather than distress human beings.

I remember a hot July afternoon in Cairo. We were waiting for our group to assemble so we could visit the magnificent Blue Mosque. Our guide and I began talking about Mohammedanism and Christianity. "We have a lot in common," he said, "We both believe that whatever is is the will of God, don't we?" A few feet from me an emaciated, diseased, poverty-stricken man was sitting on the curb.

"What does Mohammedanism say about that man?" I asked my guide.

"It simply says that this is the will of God for his life. Isn't that what you as a Christian would say also?"

"No," I answered. "We would say that the will of God for that man is health and a life of usefulness. And we would also say that society must help God give that man his chance as a human being by providing medical care, education, and encouragement."

Christian outreach is, at its root, a sustained effort to give humanity the right of way. This is the "outward" demonstration of holiness, the "inner" expression being that we love God with our whole heart. Do we love God preeminently? If so, do we demonstrate that love by showing intelligent and active concern for the well-being of others? Being actively involved in outreach to others becomes our affirmative response to the old but always searching catechetical question: Do you expect to be made perfect in love *in this life?*

The Christian community is the only group in the world charged to obey the post-resurrection command of Jesus to "make disciples of all nations" (Matthew 28:19) and also the pre-Ascension commission to "be my witnesses . . . to the end of the earth" (Acts 1:8). Keeping faith with these expectations will always be difficult.

Most Christians throughout the two-thousand-year history of the faith have lived under circumstances of oppressive tyranny. Wesley, notwithstanding his well-trained mind, found it difficult to interpret the Atonement in a way convincing to Deists (agnostics). Global missions have found it difficult to make much headway against traditional cultism and other indigenous religions. Reaching out for Christ in our own communities constantly confronts subtle and not-so-subtle opposition, because large numbers of persons engage in pursuits that merely satisfy the search for pleasure or leisure. The task of Christian missions is to commend to this fragile world the fullness of life available through the most humane of all persons, Jesus Christ.

CHRIST FOR ALL?

When we engage in Christian outreach at any level, our goal should be to represent Christ's love to all persons at all levels of life. Sadly, mainline denominations now tend to serve the "up and ins," looking a bit disdainfully on the "down and outs." The respectable middle class are those we usually seek. Love of neighbor, in the Christian sense, shows no partiality. It is not self-selective of one's own kind. Albert Outler once said that the only love he had ever trusted and felt sustained by was *from* God, *through* men and women whose love was unselfish—persons who loved him grace-fully.

So, however we may define mission and missions, they will always bring together Christian experience and Christian activity, moving always from center to circumference. From our Wesleyan beginnings we view the application of the gospel to the problems of our society as one way to demonstrate the inward transformations of grace. The problems we are called upon to address are many. Some are individualistic and relatively simple; others are entangled in our frustrating social malaise.

Among the problems currently exercising Christian and Methodist concern are the following:

The problem of inertia

Within the community of faith itself we have the problem of inertia. Experiments in physics demonstrate that inertia, a condition of inactivity, persists until some outside force intervenes. A problem that troubled Wesley was the difficulty he experienced in getting Methodists to put the principles of Christianity into practice. He faced the problem early in his own life. An entry in his first Oxford diary (dated October 1, 1726) consisted of only two words: "Idleness slays."

The urgency of the gospel calls for action as a form of witness. "Christianity in earnest" has always been Methodism's temperament. Where inertia threatens the mission of any congregation, the "outside force" of grace promises to renew the sense of urgency to carry the good news beyond the congregation.

Carelessness in speech

The problem of misusing speech seems to be everywhere. Common profanity, even among professing Christians, seems to be accepted as normal and irresistible. Have you ever noticed the striking proximity of slang and profanity? We substitute "darn" for "damn," "heck" for "hell," "gad" for "God," and so forth. Our use of bywords is hardly much better.

Language for the Christian is a sacred vehicle that communicates ideas; it also reveals something about the person who speaks. Wesley was troubled that speech was used in perverse ways. He cautioned that, should Christians see anything they could not approve, they should speak about it only to the person concerned. Christians should never speak about other persons in their absence unless they could speak well of them. We could spread immense good if our speech were always refined, indicating that we have been with Jesus. Then, too, we should be honest in our speech, and demonstrate that as Christians, our word is our bond.

Disordered family life

The problem of disordered family life, even in enlightened societies, has become prevalent and distressing. Children roam the streets of large cities and small towns aimlessly. Affluence has enabled parents to give children independent means for spending money without accountability. Exploiters of all descriptions prey on the innocent and defenseless. Love has been cheapened in meaning until it is hardly more than indulgence for a season. Marriage has become experiment instead of commitment.

The gospel cares about the family as the primary nurturing unit for helping children. Like the young Jesus, children need families to grow and become strong, full of wisdom, and enabled to enjoy the favor of both God and human beings (Luke 2:40).

"Next to your wife are your children," Wesley said to the men of his time, and he described sons and daughters as "immortal spirits whom God hath, for a time, entrusted to your care." He called this responsibility "a glorious and important trust."

We United Methodists attach more than casual importance to the development and enrichment of the Christian family. We publish special materials to help parents as well as children; we provide, at considerable expense, settings for families to share with other families in wholesome activities; we offer help of many kinds to salvage disintegrating homes. Long before the breakdown of family life became so widespread, a concern began to develop. We cannot take adult responsibilities for children too seriously. However, it is easy not to take them seriously enough. Christian parents patiently search for all the insight possible into the problems of child development. Earnest attempts to make religion sensible and joyous for children are essential.

Alcohol, drug abuse, gambling

The problems of alcohol, drug abuse, and gambling are now rampant. Christian anxiety about these problems is as old as Christianity itself. Saint Paul wrote to the Christians in Rome: "Let us conduct ourselves becomingly as in the day, not in reveling and drunkenness, not in debauchery and licentiousness. . . . But put on the Lord Jesus Christ, and make no provision for the flesh, to gratify its desires" (Romans 13:13-14).

Wesley's comment on this scripture was to the effect that Christians are not called to put on purity and sobriety, peacefulness and benevolence, but to *put on Christ.* The appeal of the gospel to those who are willing to devastate their bodies and scramble their minds by alcohol or drug abuse or to those who indulge in gambling comes out of Paul's letter to the Corinthian Christians in whose city every imaginable human indulgence was practiced: "Do you not know that your body is a temple of the Holy Spirit within you, which you have from God? You are not your own; you were bought with a price. So glorify God in your body" (1 Corinthians 6:19-20).

Wesley first became interested in problems such as these when Stephen Hales, a trustee of the Georgia Colony in America, showed him the compatibility of scientific pursuits with genuine Christian faith. Dr. Hales' pioneer inductive studies of alcohol, its effect upon the structure and functions of the human body, and its social consequences as a cause of poverty, disease, and crime gave a permanent directive to Wesley's thought and interest.

The current popularizing of alcohol, drugs, and gambling has even caused some church members to practice and defend these indulgences. Nevertheless, pastors devote large blocks of time trying to restore unfortunate victims to Christ-centered living. So prevalent are these problems that the church's only way to address them is to encourage laypersons who claim that they are governed by the constraining love of Christ (2 Corinthians 5:14) to bear consistent witness as they take their places in the world of daily work and social contacts. In no other area of human need is the quality of the Christ-centered life so influential in effecting change.

Physical, mental, and emotional disorders

Physical, mental, and emotional disorders constitute another problem. United Methodist concern in these areas of distressed living has its origin in the work of Christ. His tender healing ministries to such persons sometimes frightened those who witnessed his marvelous work.

Wesley had a sympathetic interest in such persons. He recorded in his *Journal* on May 12, 1759, an incident about a woman whose son's death caused her severe physical distress. Her physician did not diagnose the root of the disorder, but he prescribed drugs that had no effect. Wesley commented that all physicians should consider to what extent bodily disorders are caused or influenced by the mind. In those cases that are clearly out of the sphere of a physician, a pastor should be called. On the reverse side of that coin, when pastors find the mind disordered by the body, they should call in the assistance of a physician. That really was quite an enlightened observation in the 1700s.

We hear much today about ministering to the whole person. This is good Methodist theology. By and large, we have been reasonably successful in establishing working relationships among professional individuals, organizations, and agencies in order to provide comprehensive help and even extended care when necessary.

We know that many of these disorders are not yet fully understood and others do not yet have adequate treatment. So we encourage and support rigorous research into such problems, grateful for the almost miraculous strides already evident. And we dare to hope for more, much more. We do not dismiss from our thinking that God can heal mental, emotional, and physical distresses; but neither do we try to displace medical and psychological remedies with reliance on extraordinary healing. In many cases we believe that the Great Physician works through the knowledge and skills of those who are trained in dealing with these problems. Our most important spiritual service to the distressed may often be the instilling of freedom from anxiety. The patient's tranquility will often enhance the success of surgery or treatment.

Christian stewardship

Another dimension in the Methodist concern with missions is the issue of Christian stewardship. In the Genesis story God made his highest creation (Adam and Eve) responsible for tending the earth and for being attentive to the well-being of the human family. Wesley earnestly believed that Christian stewardship, working in conjunction with social service, embraces all of human life and activity. Archbishop Usher, with whose spirit and mind Wesley felt some kinship, asserted that, to be perfect, a person's heart should be aflame with the love of God, and that every thought, word, and work should be offered up to God as an acceptable spiritual sacrifice.

This description of perfection could just as well be an interpretation of Christian stewardship! This theological understanding of stewardship leads to some practical applications.

Time is precious, so long conversations are wasteful. "Do you not converse too long at a time?" Wesley asked his preachers. Then he asked another question: "Is not an hour commonly enough?" When ministerial candidates are counseled before they are admitted to Annual Conference membership, they are asked a number of questions, including: "Will you observe the following directions? Be diligent. Never be unemployed. Never be triflingly employed. Never trifle away time; neither spend any more time at any one place than is strictly necessary."

CHRISTIAN USE OF MONEY

Money must be managed with care. Wesley's sermons about riches were precise and practical. He observed that Christians had great difficulty in practicing Christian principles in handling money. Excerpts from those sermons would lead to a helpful summary for applying the gospel to the stewardship of material resources.

The first rule of prudence is "Gain all you can." We ought not to gain money at the expense of life, nor at the expense of our health. We are to gain all we can without hurting our mind. Finally, we are to gain all we can without hurting our neighbor, in substance or body. Therefore we may not sell anything that tends to impair health. Neither may we gain by hurting our neighbor in his or her soul.

The second rule of Christian prudence is, "Save all you can." Do not throw precious talent away in idle expenses. And the third rule is: "Give all you can." These rules must be applied to property ownership and management. Those who own property or manage labor possess enormous power. Christians who are cast in these roles are called to assess the use of power critically, and to seek to align this use with the principles of Christian stewardship.

OTHER SOCIETAL PROBLEMS

Now we consider some problems that distress society at large and need whatever light the Christian community and conscience can shed on them. Our backdrop is a tapestry of social reforms that were undertaken in England as the outworking of the Wesleyan Revival produced a new interpretation of philanthropy. This new attitude resulted in prison reforms, infused clemency and wisdom concerning penal laws and practices, abolished the slave trade, and opened the first doors to public education. We see problems of equal magnitude today that are just as critical and in need of the impact of the gospel.

Issues of justice

Christian conscience has played an important role in humanizing law. Some actions sanctioned by the law, the people, and even the church in the American colonies are now regarded as inhumane if not barbaric. Minorities and the poor often have a hard time getting evenhanded decisions from the courts. Issues of justice still go begging for equity.

The Christian community has demonstrated some reluctance in getting involved in attempting to correct problems of injustice. This is a volatile issue, to be sure, but society must be monitored so that the justice it administers will reflect the spirit of a sensitive, ethical, and caring community. Perhaps our hesitancy in offering Christian guidance may be explained by the increasing complexities of the legal system, or because so much has already been achieved through a considerable body of corrective legislation. Even so, some issues involving justice still remain unresolved. "New occasions" do "teach new duties."

In any case, we cannot afford to disregard Wesley's courageous stance when the laws in England were repressive. Wesley did not see how Christianity could exist without joining inward experience with outward practice of justice, mercy, and truth. This is what he called genuine morality.

Issues of humanity

Justice issues are stubborn problems to tackle. Former President Jimmy Carter tried harder than any head of state in history to focus attention on what he called "human rights." He actually made some progress in arousing global consciousness about violations against human beings. Precedents for the church's involvement in issues of humanity, like most of our social concerns, are easy to come by.

The most glaring human rights issue of Wesley's time was slavery. A member of Parliament, William Wilberforce, who had come under the influence of the Wesleyan Revival, became convinced that slavery was the worst imaginable crime against human beings. Early in his public career he began to call on Parliament to abolish the slave trade. His was an unpopular cause, for the British and the Americans defended slavery as the backbone of the economy. Wesley gave Wilberforce open encouragement and support in his daring effort. On February 24, 1791 (just a week before his death) Wesley wrote a note to the thirty-two-year-old member of Parliament, telling him he did not see how he could go through his opposition to the villainy of slavery unless God himself had raised him up for this purpose. He told him he would be worn out by the opposition of men and devils. He encouraged him by writing: "If God be for you, who can be against you?" He confidently believed that all of his adversaries put together were not stronger than God. So he challenged Wilberforce to go on in the name of God and in the power of God's might, till all slavery vanished. Wilberforce failed repeatedly, but kept on pleading his cause before Parliament. He insisted that not only should the slaves be freed but their owners should be compensated by the nation for their loss (on the grounds that the state had given its legal approval to slaveholding).

Forty-two years after Wesley's death Wilberforce himself lay dying at his home in London. The date was July 25, 1833. The House of Commons was discussing the bill for the complete abolition of slavery, including compensation to the planters of twenty million pounds. In the evening there was a knock on the door of Wilberforce's house.

"Can we see Mr. Wilberforce?"

"He is very ill."

"We bring him good news." They were taken to the room where the small figure lay upon the bed.

"Mr. Wilberforce, the Commons have passed the bill!" A wonderful smile lit up the thin face of the dying man.

"Thank God," he whispered, "that I should have lived to witness a day in which England is willing to give twenty millions sterling for the abolition of slavery!"

(Parenthetically, ratification of the Thirteenth Amendment to the United States Constitution abolishing slavery occurred thirty-two years later, on December 18, 1865.)

Deepseated problems of humanity, supported so often by politics and economics, are hard to change. But silence on the part of Christians only prolongs the agonies of the oppressed.

William Cullen Bryant's words, written during the lifetime of Wilberforce, endure:

> Truth crushed to earth shall rise again,
> The eternal years of God are hers;
> But Error, wounded, writhes in pain,
> And dies among his worshippers.

Masterpieces of Religious Verse, James Dalton Morrison, ed.

The issues of humanity today are just as formidable and repressive as the slavery issue was in the 1800s. The buildup of nuclear overkill by super powers, the huddling of families in ghettos, political oppression, mind control—who can deny the presence of these issues in our global society? Who can rest content until they are dealt with? Bringing the mind and spirit of Christ to bear upon such problems for the sake of humanity may be a task for angels; but it has been entrusted to the community of the reconciled—to us!

Issues of social inequities

The great gulf between the haves and the have-nots seems to be widening, perhaps because the world population is exploding faster than resources to sustain it can be developed. Even in the United States periodic government reports shock us with statistics revealing increases in the number of persons living below the poverty line. Christians, faithful to their trust, are disturbed about poverty and its attendant evils. That the problem is persistent can be documented. A person caught in the cycle of poverty finds it almost impossible to get out.

The plight of the poor

Jesus was distressed at the plight of the poor. Wesley was so troubled by it that he repeatedly inveighed against it. Poverty, he observed, makes a person liable to be laughed at. He made the observation that many persons toil, and labor, and sweat to have food. They struggle with weariness and hunger together. After a hard day's labor, a man returns to a poor, cold, dirty, uncomfortable lodging, and finds no food to restore his wasted strength. He told those who lived at ease that they needed only eyes to see, ears to hear, and hearts to understand how well God had dealt with them. He asked them what it would be like to seek bread day by day and find none. Worse yet, what about the father of five or six children who cried for the food he could not give them? Who can tell what it means to want for bread, he asked, unless one has felt that same hunger? Human poverty is brutalizing.

We can thank God when Christians respond to aid victims of famine and other disasters. There is still so much to do, however, and Jesus' example compels us to action. Whatever we are doing, even sporadically, does say that we really want to put our hearts and hands to tasks of ameliorating human misery.

The sick and dying

Inequities also persist in the area of making medications and treatment available to the sick. We are distressed when telecasts show us victims of treatable diseases going untreated because we cannot seem to muster the necessary delivery systems. How many vials of antibiotics could be dispensed for the cost of one nuclear warhead? We get quite emotional about saving the world from atomic holocaust, and well we should, but Christians should be just as distraught over the tens of thousands of human beings who are dying needlessly for want of simple nutrition and relatively inexpensive medications.

Issues of national decadence

Wesley spoke boldly of his beloved England as a guilty land, perishing in its iniquity. In every edition of the daily newspaper we read about corruption in government, graft, and bribery; about persons in business who mismanage funds to gain personal advantage; about large quantities of illegal drugs being smuggled into the United States from nations that continually appeal for and accept American aid; about education at all levels that shortchanges the minds of youth and young adults. No community can be isolated from the tragedy of national decay. When Christians lift up their voices, it must be on the side of virtue, and those voices must be lifted up fearlessly and relentlessly.

These representative issues, personal and social, help to focus why Christians insist on reaching out to the world beyond the church. An occasional victory over any of these aggravations, however modest, gives us heart. It brings God's kingdom on earth a little closer.

A delightful little story from England helps to focus this concern in another way. "You seem a very temperate people here and in comfortable circumstances," said Cardinal Newman on a walking tour in Cornwall to a miner wom he met on the way. "How do you account for it?" The miner, slowly lifting his hat, made answer: "There came a man amongst us once. His name was John Wesley." Maybe in your community a similar good word of gratitude is being spoken because of the presence there of United Methodists and other socially concerned Christians.

In offering the gospel to the world beyond the church we realize that an emotion that comes from nowhere and leads nowhere is of scant value, but a devotion that yields kind and loving deeds is abundantly worthwhile.

CHAPTER SIX

"TRAVELING HOME TO GOD"

ohn Cennick, befriended by John Wesley, was a product of the Wesleyan Revival and, for a time, taught the children of miners and served as a lay preacher. Two of his hymns remain in our hymnody: the familiar "Be Present at Our Table, Lord" and the somewhat less familiar "Children of the Heavenly King."

> Children of the heavenly King,
> As we journey let us sing;
> Sing our Savior's worthy praise,
> Glorious in his works and ways.
>
> We are traveling home to God,
> In the way our fathers trod;
> They are happy now, and we
> Soon their happiness shall see.
> *The Book of Hymns,* p. 300

Christians are necessarily and continually involved in seeing and meeting needs of this present world, but they also know that a faith without a future beyond the temporary here-and-now would never satisfy the longings of the human spirit. Adolph Harnack, a highly respected German theologian, believed that the most critical issues of Christian thought focus not on a contest between miracles and science, but rather on questions such as whether our personal life has an eternal value that distinguishes it from all else, whether or not moral

55

goodness is a life-principle of the spirit in absolute control of the universe, and whether or not there is a living and saving God.

What we believe about the future depends on what we believe about God's self-revelation in Christ, especially his triumph over death, and what we believe about the moral nature of God and the universe. Methodism has always held that the pursuit of eternal values is the great business of living. Wesley was persuaded that all children of God have had, at some time, life and death set before them—eternal life and eternal death. All have had occasion to respond to grace.

WHAT IS THE CHIEF END OF HUMANITY?

We seldom use the catechism for instructing children in church membership, but copies of the catechism are still available. One of the questions is still important: What is the chief end of man? The catechism answer was: "The chief end of man is to love God and enjoy him forever." Wesley, an Anglican who would have known the catechism, may have had this question in mind when he asked, "Why were we sent into the world?" His answer was this: "For one sole end, and no other, to prepare for eternity." Created in God's own image, our ultimate purpose as God's creation is to know, love, enjoy, and serve our Creator to all eternity. We are born for nothing else. We live for nothing else. We were not created to please our senses, to gratify our imagination, to gain money, or to receive the praise of others. Each of us must continually say: "This one thing I do, I press on to the mark." We are encouraged to pursue the enjoyment of God in time and eternity.

God works, even in this present world, in ways that differ from the way human beings work. Our ascent is slow, but God's patience with us seems to be infinite. We try to gain advantage by force; God exercises power by love.

When I stood amid the postwar rubble of London in 1951, all around Saint Paul's Cathedral I saw nothing but total devastation. Only the cathedral had been spared by the Luftwaffe's blitz. Across the European continent, from Le Havre to Rome, cities and countryside lay in ruin. God does not work to that kind of an end. God engages in the tougher business of changing human hearts to make reconciliation and healing possible.

Lincoln dedicated the Gettysburg battlefield on November 19, 1863, six months after the three days of fighting there inflicted almost 50,000 casualties. When I was there that field was covered with a carpet of beautiful green grass. God, through nature, changed the scene. Deep in the human heart must surely be some sort of yearning to develop a partnership so we can make God's better way our way.

DEPENDENT CREATURES

That longing is lodged in us because we are "children of the heavenly king." Wesley saw that the necessity of the Atonement (the sacrifice of God's Son for us) arose out of the disorder of our personal lives. We are creatures dependent on the Creator. Made in the image of God, the very crown of Creation, even the worst ravages of sin do not render us incapable of restoration by the grace of God. Wesley confessed that it was hard for him, in the light of his understanding of the gospel, to ever despair of anyone.

God never gives up on us, even though we turn away from his mercy and goodness. It should disturb us as much as it troubled Wesley that our idea about divine mercy is "unwieldy." We live as if Christ came to save his people *in,* not *from,* their sins. Some even talk about repenting by and by, taking it for granted that they can antici-pate and determine the date of their death. Others entertain the notion that good works are of no importance once reconciliation has been experienced. When Wesley was asked, "Are works necessary to the continuance of faith?" he replied that a person may *forfeit* the free gift of God (reconciliation) both by sins of commission, and by those of omission. He had no interest in the "once-saved-always-saved" notion.

TRYING TO OUT-THINK GOD

We occasionally read about someone who tries to set a time when this world will reach its end. Such speculation crops up periodically. On February 28, 1763, Wesley wrote this entry in his *Journal:*

"Preaching in the evening at Spitalfields on 'Prepare to meet thy God,' I largely showed the utter absurdity of the supposition that the world was to end that night. But notwithstanding all I could say, many were afraid to go to bed, and some wandered about in the fields, being persuaded that, if the world did not end, at least London would be swallowed up by an earthquake. I went to bed at my usual time, and was fast asleep by ten o'clock"(*The Works of John Wesley,* Vol. III, p. 130).

How presumptuous of any mortal to try to outthink God! We prove that we are "children of the heavenly king" when we let God lead us all the way and do not try to force God's hand. Isaiah 55:8-9 provides caution enough to keep us sensitive to the superior work of providence:

> My thoughts are not your thoughts,
> neither are your ways my ways, says the LORD.
> For as the heavens are higher than the earth,
>   so are my ways higher than your ways
>   and my thoughts than your thoughts.

The more we seek to know and follow God's ways here on earth the more joyful becomes our journey from the temporal to the eternal, from the mortal to the celestial.

LIMITATIONS OF OUR MORTALITY

Hungers of the human spirit—the aching heart, the empty void, the incomplete testimony, the unfinished work of God in us—are never fully satisfied here on earth no matter how closely we may become identified with God. Wesley said he never used the phrase "sinless perfection" because he was quite sure that ignorance and mistakes are inseparable from our mortality. Because of our rebellion against God, even though restoration may be achieved, we cannot avoid falling into innumerable mistakes. Consequently, we cannot always avoid wrong affections, neither can we always think, speak, and act appropriately. Our personal, individual yearnings make us know that, as Wesley put it, "Sin does not reign, but it does remain." Pride and self-will fight against us long and hard, the battle lasting even to the close of our mortal years.

We also hunger for wisdom. Christians should always be open to instruction, eager to be wiser today than we were yesterday and to change whatever we can for the better. Not what we know but how we love holds the key to cure what Paul Sabatier, the French theologian, called "homesickness for holiness." Perhaps we could make some longed-for spiritual gains if we attached more importance to the doctrine of holiness. We choose mostly to ignore it as unattainable. Or we ridicule it because it has been misrepresented by some persons who claim it, but whose expression of it turns out to be objectionable.

DAILY PRAYER AND READING

Our unsatisfied hungers will not be met as long as we seek spiritual sustenance from supernatural dreams or visions or sudden impulses. Staple daily nourishment will be found at an altogether different table. Characteristically practical about such matters, Wesley commended to others what he himself rigorously practiced: prayer and reading. He told his people that they were greatly wanting in following these practices. But he insisted that without them they could never grow in grace. Just as a child needs food for growth, so the soul must be faithfully nourished by private prayer and inspirational reading. At long last, in the grand transition when the perishable puts on the imperishable and the mortal puts on immortality (1 Corinthians 15:53), the soul's hungers that are not fully satisfied in this present world will be fully met.

So in our continuing pilgrimage we lean more and more on God, seeing with ever-clearer vision that those who want to live *with* God in the kingdom of heaven must live *to* God in the kingdom on earth. We increasingly realize, as Wesley did, that we are now more ashamed of our best duties than we were formerly of our worst sins. By this confession we admit our helplessness. So with renewed diligence we open up our total life more and more to God for every good thought, and word, and work.

If separation occurs after reconciliation, it will not be God who deserts us, but we who desert God. Grace will never compel our loyalty any more than grace forced our repentance, but the Creator offers generously all that is needed to sustain our faithfulness. In faithfulness God is all-gracious. As the Preserver of life, as well as its Creator, God remains everywhere present. God's own self-giving to us and our response produce a very special result. Wesley found out in his own life that God breathed into him every good desire, and brought every good desire to good effect. He knew and felt that the very first motion of good was from above, as well as the power to carry through to action. God not only infuses every good desire, but sustains us in a whole way of life.

We must recognize and acknowledge our shortcomings. But certainly that is not where we stop. We think about all those whose faith and faithfulness sustained them when they were victimized by tyranny, not just in times long gone but even now. In many ways the world is unfriendly to those who want to live as sons and daughters of God, but we can still find good reason to sing:

> This is my Father's world,
> And to my listening ears
> All nature sings, and round me rings
> The music of the spheres.
>
> .   .   .   .
>
> This is my father's world:
> He shines in all that's fair;
> In the rustling grass I hear him pass;
> He speaks to me everywhere.
>
> This is my Father's world.
> O let me ne'er forget
> That though the wrong seems oft so strong,
> God is the ruler yet . . .
>
> .   .   .   .
>
> The Lord is King: let the heavens ring!
> God reigns; let the earth be glad!
>
> *The United Methodist Hymnal,* 144

How like these sentiments was Wesley's assessment of this present world, despite all the miseries that prevailed in his own land. In his later years he wrote a thoughtful discourse to show the more excellent way amid an extreme pessimism that condemns the present age as "the dregs of time" and locates the golden age in long-lost antiquity. Nor did he endorse the mindless optimism that looks upon the past as "an immense sea of errors," that despaired of the present, and that located the golden age just over the crest of the hill in some great tomorrow. Wesley held the conviction that human progress is not fiction, but fact—not a dream but a reality. He noted changes that marked his age as excelling all former times: its advance in the knowledge of nature (a reference to the beginnings of the scientific movement) and the triumph in religion of toleration (a reference to the special infuence of the Enlightenment).

Our mortality and our temporary earthbound existence may somewhat hinder the vitality of our immortal spirit, but the struggles of the soul are not without merit. We are in a world that tests what we do with our freedom. We are free to choose in every moment between good and evil, to serve God or fall prey to satanic influences. When we choose the good and God, we have the assistance of divine grace; when we serve evil and the Adversary, the most we can expect is short-lived and superficial sensual gratification.

The victories we win as we go on in our God-directed journey give us a foretaste of the heavenly state. Wesley concluded that eternal life begins when it pleases God to reveal the Son in our hearts. Then happiness begins—real, solid, substantial happiness. Then the heavenly state commences for us. While we steadfastly look, not at the things that are seen, but at those that are not seen, we are more and more separated from the world. When the eye of the soul becomes fixed on things that are not temporal but eternal, our affections become more and more detached from earth, and fixed on things above. That lively faith is the most direct and effective means of promoting righteousness and true holiness—of establishing the holy and spiritual law in the believer's heart.

As the transition from our earthbound state to life everlasting draws closer we follow in the train of our Christian forebears who died singing. The early Methodists called this "dying well." The hymn Wesley tried to sing on his dying day was:

> I'll praise my Maker while I've breath;
> And when my voice is lost in death,
> Praise shall employ my nobler powers.
> My days of praise shall ne'er be past,
> While life, and thought, and being last,
> Or immortality endures.
>
> *The United Methodist Hymnal,* 60

CHRISTIAN JOY

The children of God do travel "along life's toilsome way," but joyfulness is their prevailing mood and disposition. There is nothing superficial about Christian joy. Our longing for happiness reaches out toward a sovereign power that cares about us. It is good news that God so loved the world that he gave his only Son to the world in order that we might not perish but have eternal life.

The Christian gospel is the message of God's suffering, redeeming, reconciling love that calls us to new life in Christ. All believers do not possess the same quality and fullness of emotion at all times, but faith itself has a distinctive emotional tone when viewed over time.

Evil entices us to seek all happiness here and now. The Christian rejects that appeal on the grounds that deep and abiding happiness can be found only in the Creator. The divine happiness God shares with us is full and permanent.

Christ's joy stayed with him all the way, even through his crucifixion (Hebrews 12:2). He took the burdens and sorrows of those who responded to him and turned them into invitations to find joy in commitment to divine obedience.

CHRISTIAN PEACE AND POWER

Yet another foretaste of the life to come is the Christian's experience of peace and power. Evangelist Billy Graham commented once that most of those who come forward in his crusades express a need for assurance. This response reflects how difficult it is for many in our popular culture to understand the deeper process which Wesley called the "witness of the Spirit."

The "witness of the Spirit," for Wesley, implied both an immediate event (e.g., the knowledge of justifying grace), and a process through time (i.e., sanctifying grace). The presence of the Spirit in both the event and the process also implied, however, that all of God's provision and promise are present to the believer, as history (memory) and promise (hope). In this sense, Christianity is a present-tense religion. We all know numerous New Testament affirmations such as these: "Our inner nature *is* being renewed day by day. . . . We believe, and so we speak. . . . If any one *is* in Christ, he *is* a new creation. . . . *Now* is the acceptable time; behold *now* is the day of salvation. . . . Do you not realize that Jesus Christ *is* in you? . . . You are no longer a slave but a son. . . . Christ has set us free. . . . He *is* our peace. . . . Let your manner of life be worthy of the gospel of Christ. . . . God *is* at work in you, both to will and to work for his good pleasure." Our "now" faith brings the peace and power of God into everyday relationships.

Of ourselves we have no merit to earn reconciliation; of ourselves we have no strength to bring holy influences to bear on our age. So it is God's doing, but only when we give God that opportunity do we rest content. We then come into harmony with the Creator's world around us; we look within and find we are in harmony with the Creator's spirit. The assurance, peace, and power we enjoy represent God at work in our favor. God's continuing presence through the years of our life on earth will not be interrupted as long as we choose and cherish all that God desires for us. Wesley, citing Paul's testimony before King Agrippa ("I was not disobedient to the heavenly vision," Acts 26:19), told his listeners not to look for peace within until they were at peace with God. God does give meaning, joy, and hope to our lives. It is God's love in us that can make us secure and serene. All of life's final meanings are in God's hands.

This is the good news: God is on our side (Romans 8:31). Certain words of the Apostle Paul, originally addressed to his most loyal friends, the Philippian Christians, speak just as helpfully to us: "Have no anxiety about anything, but in everything by prayer and supplication with thanksgiving let your requests be made known to God. And the peace of God, which passes all understanding, will keep your hearts and your minds in Christ Jesus" (Philippians 4:6-7).

The Creator of the moral universe acts freely in accordance with the divine laws set to govern the universe. God will not act whimsically or show partiality. As persons we are endowed by God with moral sensitivity. We can distinguish between good and evil, right and wrong, hate and love. So, through the activity of conscience ("an inward check," Wesley called it), we know that God's judgment is at work in us here and now. God's mercy is available to those who diligently seek to do God's will. But unresolved guilt cannot go unchallenged at last. The reconciled person thrills to the words of "And Can It Be That I Should Gain," the hymn written by Charles Wesley recalling his own experience of reconciliation:

> No condemnation now I dread;
> Jesus, and all in him, is mine;
> Alive in him, my living Head,
> And clothed in righteousness divine,
> Bold I approach th'eternal throne,
> And claim the crown, through Christ my own.
>
> *The United Methodist Hymnal,* 363

God's overtures toward us are so generous and the Spirit's efforts to kindle our love are so constant, that we realize God would take no delight in condemning us. We condemn ourselves. Wesley saw God's tender goodness even in the imposition of God's justice. He discerned that God may reward more, but will never punish more, than strict justice requires. God will not punish anyone for doing anything that could not possibly be avoided, nor for omitting anything which could not possibly be done.

NO GOD-GIVEN LICENSE TO SIN

We may try to rationalize even deliberate lapses in righteousness on the supposition that God would not be disturbed over some compromises. Wesley made the point that no one should ever infer from God's long-suffering spirit that we have been given a license to sin. Continuing in sin because of God's extraordinary divine mercy is folly. Those who persist in sin, presuming that God will save them at the last, will be miserably disappointed.

Wesley also cautioned against letting self-certainty (one of his ongoing battles with predestination) obscure the need for constant monitoring of one's thoughts and deeds to submit them to the control of the mind and spirit of Christ. Anyone can fall away, even those who perceive themselves to be holy or righteous in the judgment of God. Those who are endued with the faith that purifies the heart and produces a good conscience, who are grafted into the spiritual and invisible church, who so effectively know Christ that they can escape the pollutions of the world, who see the light of the glory of God in the face of Jesus Christ, who live by faith in the Son of God—persons of such evident commitment should be especially mindful of Paul's admonition: "Let any one who thinks that he stands take heed lest he fall" (1 Corinthians 10:12).

BEYOND THIS EARTHLY LIFE

Some think this earthly life is all we can count on. After death, they say, is oblivion. Such a notion runs counter to the character of the moral universe. If that were true, inequities would never be fairly adjudicated. The moral law and the moral universe would collapse. Those who stood at the brink of martyrdom, who suffered much abuse and pain in this life, received words of uncommon encouragement and hope from one of the early fathers of the church: "He [God] will wipe away every tear from their eyes, and death shall be no more, neither shall there be mourning nor crying nor pain any more, for the former things have passed away" (Revelation 21:4).

We celebrate the Christian hope. The gospel lets us know that we can live intentionally, that we can follow the inner leadings of the Holy Spirit, that we can obey what we are given to know of God's will, growing all the time into deeper faith and truer happiness. Jesus Christ, having revealed God's love for us, constantly renews us as God's children.

CONCLUSION

n an age caught up in secular pursuits, the church as God's agency for offering new life to the world must unlock the riches of the good news and offer it as lavishly as possible upon all who yearn for something more than what they find elsewhere. Our human predicament is no different from that in the age addressed by Wesley. He looked upon the world as a mighty flood of human wickedness with only a trickling stream of human goodness.

We experience consternation when we know that millions of persons will not attain any considerable achievements of either mind or spirit in their lifetimes. What is the response of the Body of Christ to the call and cry of the world?

Christian thought, songs, and sermons in all ages furnish convincing evidence that we *receive* the gospel when we pray, "God, be merciful to me a sinner"; we *experience* it when the Spirit bears witness to our spirit; and we *live* it when we humbly declare: "I can do all things in him [Christ] who strengthens me" (Philippians 4:13).

As we observe decadence around us, we also see that we cannot escape from becoming a church engaged in some form of continuous revival. Since the beginning of the Christian era the hub of the church's evangelical witness has been the pulpit, made vibrant when those who preach the good news proclaim it both from experience and conviction.

We do well to remember that Wesley's preaching after his conversion experience changed his hitherto feeble, unproductive utterances into preaching that Wesley himself said "ran as fire in dry stubble." His became the kind of proclamation, both in substance and style, that brought the full prophetic Christian ideal and standards of life to bear upon the half-heathen religion and morality of his age. He forced his hearers to look into the chasm between nominal Christianity and the real Christianity of Jesus. When they lived the faith they didn't need to explain it. It was a self-proving, self-evident faith lifestyle.

So all persons, clergy and laity alike, are called upon to build each other up in the faith. We are shepherds who tend the lambs and go before the flock to guide them in all the ways of truth and holiness. We nourish them with words of eternal life. We feed them with the pure milk of the Word. We watch over their souls as those who shall give account to God.

As difficult as the task may be at times, the sharing of the good news is nothing less than joyous privilege. A hymn of fervent enthusiasm that Charles Wesley wrote "to be sung in a tumult" by Methodists who were being persecuted and even assaulted, provides a fitting summary:

> Ye servants of God, your Master proclaim,
> And publish abroad his wonderful name;
> The name all-victorious of Jesus extol,
> His kingdom is glorious and rules over all.
>
> God ruleth on high, almighty to save,
> And still he is nigh, his presence we have;
> The great congregation his triumph shall sing,
> Ascribing salvation to Jesus, our King.
>
> "Salvation to God, who sits on the throne!"
> Let all cry aloud and honor the Son;
> The praises of Jesus the angels proclaim,
> Fall down on their faces and worship the Lamb.
>
> Then let us adore, and give him his right,
> All glory and power, all wisdom and might;
> All honor and blessing with angels above,
> And thanks never ceasing and infinite love.

The United Methodist Hymnal, 181

BIBLIOGRAPHY

PRIMARY SOURCES

Wesley, John. *Sermons on Several Occasions*. London: The Epworth Press, 1950.

_____. *The Journal of the Reverend John Wesley, A.M.* 4 Vol., London: Everyman's Library.

_____. *Explanatory Notes upon the New Testament*. London: The Epworth Press, 1958.

_____. *Christian Perfection*. Cleveland, Ohio: The World Publishing Co., 1954.

SECONDARY SOURCES

Burtner, Robert W. and Robert E. Chiles, eds. *John Wesley's Theology*. Nashville: Abingdon Press, 1982.

Cell, George Croft. *The Rediscovery of John Wesley*. New York: Henry Holt and Co., 1935.

McConnell, Francis J. *The Essentials of Methodism*. New York: The Methodist Book Concern, 1916.

Northcott, Cecil. *All God's Chillun*. London: Edinburgh House Press, 1941.

Outler, Albert C. *Theology In the Wesleyan Spirit*. Nashville: Discipleship Resources-Tidings, 1975.

The Book of Worship. Nashville: The Methodist Publishing House, 1965.

The Encyclopedia Americana. 30 Vol. New York: Encyclopedia Americana Corp., 1946.

The New Testament, (RSV). New York: Thomas Nelson and Sons, 1946.

The United Methodist Book of Hymns. Nashville: The Methodist Publishing House, 1966.

The United Methodist Hymnal. Nashville: The United Methodist Publishing House, 1989.

Discipleship Resources
Subscription Service

50 % OFF

Get $60.00 worth of books
for just $30.00!
And *SAVE 20%*
on each additional copy you order
of the selected resource!

For **just $30.00** we will mail you from one to four books every other month for a full year.

All titles are developed and/ or approved by the program sections of **The General Board of Discipleship.**

DISCIPLESHIP RESOURCES
MATERIALS FOR GROWTH IN CHRISTIAN FAITH AND LIFE
P.O. Box 189 • Nashville, TN 37202 • Phone (615) 340-7285

☐ *Yes, please enroll me...or the church named below...in Discipleship Resources Subscription Service for one year.*
—— *Payment Enclosed ...U.S. Funds only*
—— *Please Bill Me ... Account #* ———————
                                      IF KNOWN
T07

Bill to: ————————————————————

Billing Address: ————————————————

City/St/Zp: ——————————————————

Send to: ————————————————————

Mailing Address: ————————————————

City/St/Zp: ——————————————————